DEALING WITH
TEEN PREGNANCY

By Emily Mahoney

Portions of this book originally appeared in *Teen Pregnancy* by Jenny MacKay.

LUCENT
PRESS

Published in 2017 by
Lucent Press, an Imprint of Greenhaven Publishing, LLC
353 3rd Avenue
Suite 255
New York, NY 10010

Designer: Deanna Paternostro
Editor: Jennifer Lombardo

Library of Congress Cataloging-in-Publication Data

Names: Mahoney, Emily, author.
Title: Teen pregnancy / Emily Mahoney.
Description: New York : Lucent Press, [2017] | Series: Hot topics | Includes
 bibliographical references and index.
Identifiers: LCCN 2016046973 (print) | LCCN 2016049480 (ebook) | ISBN
 9781534560192 (library bound) | ISBN 9781534560208 (E-book)
Subjects: LCSH: Teenage mothers. | Teenage pregnancy. | Youth–Sexual
 behavior.
Classification: LCC HQ759.4 .M364 2017 (print) | LCC HQ759.4 (ebook) | DDC
 306.874/3–dc23
LC record available at https://lccn.loc.gov/2016046973

Printed in the United States of America

CPSIA compliance information: Batch #CW17KL: For further information contact Greenhaven Publishing LLC, New York,
New York at 1-844-317-7404.

Please visit our website, www.greenhavenpublishing.com. For a free color catalog of all our
high-quality books, call toll free 1-844-317-7404 or fax 1-844-317-7405.

CONTENTS

Adolescence is a time when many people begin to take notice of the world around them. News channels, blogs, and talk radio shows are constantly promoting one view or another; very few are unbiased. Young people also hear conflicting information from parents, friends, teachers, and acquaintances. Often, they will hear only one side of an issue or be given flawed information. People who are trying to support a particular viewpoint may cite inaccurate facts and statistics on their blogs, and news programs present many conflicting views of important issues in our society. In a world where it seems everyone has a platform to share their thoughts, it can be difficult to find unbiased, accurate information about important issues.

It is not only facts that are important. In blog posts, in comments on online videos, and on talk shows, people will share opinions that are not necessarily true or false, but can still have a strong impact. For example, many young people struggle with their body image. Seeing or hearing negative comments about particular body types online can have a huge effect on the way someone views himself or herself and may lead to depression and anxiety. Although it is important not to keep information hidden from young people under the guise of protecting them, it is equally important to offer encouragement on issues that affect their mental health.

The titles in the Hot Topics series provide readers with different viewpoints on important issues in today's society. Many of these issues, such as teen pregnancy and Internet safety, are of immediate concern to young people. This series aims to give readers factual context on these crucial topics in a way that lets them form their own opinions. The facts presented throughout also serve to empower readers to help themselves or support people they know who are struggling with many of the challenges adolescents face today. Although negative viewpoints are not ignored or downplayed, this series allows young people to see that the challenges they face are not insurmountable. Eating disorders can be overcome, the Internet can be navigated safely, and pregnant teens do not have to feel hopeless.

Quotes encompassing all viewpoints are presented and cited so readers can trace them back to their original source, verifying for themselves whether the information comes from a reputable place. Additional books and websites are listed, giving readers a starting point from which to continue their own research. Chapter questions encourage discussion, allowing young people to hear and understand their classmates' points of view as they further solidify their own. Full-color photographs and enlightening charts provide a deeper understanding of the topics at hand. All of these features augment the informative text, helping young people understand the world they live in and formulate their own opinions concerning the best way they can improve it.

A Social Problem on the Decline

In the 1990s, pregnancy rates were at an all-time high in the United States for unmarried teenagers. The Centers for Disease Control and Prevention (CDC) reported that in 1990, "there were an estimated 1 million pregnancies and 521,626 births to U.S. women aged 15-19 years."[1] This represents an estimated pregnancy rate of about 118 per 1,000 women and an estimated birth rate of about 60 per 1,000 women. The number of pregnancies includes girls who became pregnant but then had either an abortion or a miscarriage. Teen pregnancy is considered a serious problem in society because it can negatively affect the lives of the teen mothers, teen fathers, and their new children. Teen parents often find it difficult to continue going to school, which can affect their job prospects. Many teen parents, especially those without strong family support, have trouble supporting themselves and their children financially. These issues cause a lot of stress for teen families, which can make it difficult for the parents to stay together and can negatively affect their physical and mental health.

Fortunately, the rate of teen pregnancy has decreased since 1990. Many believe one reason for this decline is that the issue has become more widely discussed in the media. Nonetheless, there is little consensus about the best way to help America's teens avoid having children before they are ready. Abstinence and safe-sex programs are hotly debated. Americans also do not agree about how best to help teens cope with the situation if they do become pregnant and are facing the options of abortion, adoption, or keeping the baby. The varied opinions on these issues are often in the spotlight as the media frequently reports on teen pregnancy, and television shows such as MTV's *16 and*

Although the teen pregnancy rate has been steadily falling, many teens still become pregnant.

Pregnant, *Teen Mom*, and *Teen Mom 2* have drawn increased media attention to this controversial issue. Teen pregnancy has been a hot topic in social, health, educational, and political arenas in the United States for several generations, but public opinions about the issue remain widely varied.

Teen pregnancy has not always been so closely examined. Before the 1960s, it was generally considered wrong only if a young woman became pregnant before she was married. Pregnancy that did occur before marriage often resulted in a quickly planned wedding, even between teenagers. During the 1960s, however, American attitudes about sexual activity before marriage began to change. During a wave of support for feminism and women's rights, people started objecting to the double standard that caused women who had premarital sex to face more serious physical consequences and social prejudices than their male partners. The birth control pill also came on the market in the 1960s. This pill provides a dose of hormones that a woman takes daily to avoid an unplanned pregnancy. For the first time in history, women could now prevent child-bearing by a means other than abstinence, and they began to think differently about sex. By the 1970s and 1980s, unmarried women and men of all ages had launched a sexual revolution. The sexual practices of Americans changed as women, men, and teenagers felt freer to explore sexual relationships outside of marriage.

The occurrence of unplanned pregnancy, especially among teens, did not vanish with the invention of new birth control methods, however. In fact, the teen pregnancy rate in America began to climb steeply in the 1970s and 1980s, hitting the highest rates in recorded American history. This sparked public concern about the sexual morality of teenagers, the effectiveness of birth control medication, and the problem of children being born to women who were considered too young to raise them. It was also during this period—in 1973—that abortion was made legal in the United States. Teen abortion rates began to climb along with the rate of teen pregnancy, which set off more public concern that young women were using abortion as after-the-fact birth control, choosing to terminate their pregnancies instead of preventing them in the first place. By the late 1980s, American society considered teen pregnancy one of the nation's most worrisome problems.

The teen pregnancy rate peaked in the United States in 1990. Then, for the next 10 years, the annual number of teens who became pregnant began a steep and steady decline. The efforts of groups and agencies working to reduce teen pregnancy seemed successful. However, during the early 2000s, the decline leveled off, and in 2006, the teen pregnancy rate rose by 3 percent, which caused renewed concern that nationwide strategies to reduce teen pregnancy had begun to fail. In recent years, though, the rate has gone down, and in 2014, the rate of births to females ages 15 to 19 was 24.2 per 1000, which was down from 26.5 per 1000 in 2013. Despite this encouraging trend, the United States still has a teen pregnancy rate higher than any other country in the industrialized world. Teen pregnancy remains one of the major issues confronting American society today.

What Causes Teen Pregnancy?

In 2014, a total of 249,078 babies were born to women ages 15 to 19 years in the United States, and approximately 3 in 10 teenage girls will become pregnant by the time they are 20 years old. About 60 percent of teenage pregnancies result in live births. Many teens who become pregnant have not completed high school; the average age of high school graduates is 18. Teen mothers face many challenges because many of them lack a high school diploma, without which it is almost impossible to get a job that pays enough to support a family. Dropping out of high school is related to a number of negative outcomes. For example, the median income of people ages 18 through 67 who had not completed high school was roughly $25,000 in 2009. By comparison, the median income of people ages 18 through 67 who completed their education with at least a high school credential, including a General Educational Development (GED) certificate, was approximately $43,000.[2] Because of this, children born to teenage mothers are more likely to be raised in a financially struggling family.

Teen pregnancy is not only an economic and personal issue; it affects society as well. The way that children are raised and the structure of what constitutes a family are issues that are frequently discussed because of their importance to society. Who gives birth to children and who raises children are questions at the forefront of many political discussions because of the effects that the way a child is raised can have on society. Raising well-balanced, emotionally stable children who will become productive members of society requires a huge investment of time and resources, both from parents and the community. Children born to teen parents who are not yet emotionally mature and prepared to raise them may suffer disadvantages that affect not only them as individuals, but also the community to which they belong.

Because teen pregnancy trends have potentially negative effects on the future of American culture, both socially and financially, it is important to understand why many American teens are making choices that lead to pregnancy. Changing American values are often blamed. American teens get pregnant at a much higher rate than teens in other countries, despite the fact that the pregnancy rate in America is much lower than in years past. This raises concerns that America's teens are irresponsible and not adequately prepared for adulthood. There is also controversy over whether teenagers' moral values are truly in question or whether American society is simply not tolerant or understanding of sexual relationships among teens, especially outside of marriage. Some of America's teens may also get pregnant in part because society portrays parenthood as a positive life event for adults. With such a complex issue, there are many different viewpoints to discuss.

The Moral Side of the Problem

Many Americans who have conservative social views believe pregnancy among teens is a sign that America's morals have changed for the worse in the past several decades. Many conservative Americans believe sex is a much more common teen behavior now than it was 50 to 60 years ago and an indication that society's moral values, particularly sexual values, are in a state of decline. According to a Gallup Poll in 2015, "When asked whether the 'state of moral values in the country as a whole is getting better or worse,' 72 percent [of Americans] polled said that they believe that the paradigm is worsening, while, in contrast, just 22 percent said that it is improving."[3] Some who claim that America's moral values are declining say teen pregnancy results from a society that has come to prize sexual freedom instead of sexual modesty and responsibility. The nonprofit organization Probe Ministries

International has focused on preserving traditional values among Christians. Kerby Anderson, president of the organization, said, "Sexually liberal elites have hijacked our culture." Sexual liberalism, Anderson said, has "transformed the social landscape of America and made promiscuity a virtue and virginity a 'problem' to be solved."[4]

If American society truly is exposing teens to more sexual ideas at younger ages, it may also be pushing them to explore sexual activity earlier in life. Even teenagers have commented on this trend. In an interview with *Good Morning America* in 2008, 14-year-old Caroline Jenks said, "It seems like our generation has matured ... sexually faster than generations previous to us."[5] This sexual "maturity" is often flaunted when teens increasingly talk about and act on sexual impulses with little modesty or consideration of the consequences. Some Americans believe that casual, meaningless sex has become a common behavior for teens in America, and there is concern that today's teens may care more about their immediate moods and feelings than about their future, education, and moral values. Teen pregnancy is one potentially negative consequence of this impulsive teen behavior. Among those concerned are many teenagers themselves. "Kids should not be worrying about 'I have to get diapers for my baby,' when I'm 16, 17 years old,"[6] a 15-year-old boy told *Good Morning America*.

Challenging Claims of Moral Decline

Not all Americans agree that American society is losing its moral values, however, or that sexual activity among teens is any more common now than in decades past. In fact, teenage birth rates have actually declined overall since the 1950s. Citing numbers from a teen pregnancy study performed by the Guttmacher Institute, an organization that researches sexual and reproductive health worldwide, teen pregnancy researchers Saul D. Hoffman and Rebecca A. Maynard said even though a long decline in the pregnancy rate among American teens ages 15 to 19 leveled off between 2005 and 2006, that year nevertheless marked "the lowest rate ever

Popularizing Pregnancy?

In 2009, MTV first aired the popular television show *16 and Pregnant*. This show documented the struggles of different teenagers who became pregnant around the age of 16. Each story followed the journey of a teenage girl for five to seven months of her pregnancy and detailed the struggles of working and attending school while pregnant, her family and friends' reactions to the pregnancy announcement, and the difficulty of raising a baby while still in high school. The show documented how the girls had to give up their lives in order to care for their children. The show ended in 2014, but spinoff series *Teen Mom OG*, *Teen Mom 2*, and *Teen Mom 3* further follow selected girls' stories as they raise their babies through toddlerhood and childhood. Many people criticized MTV for airing the shows because they believed MTV was making young girls believe that if they got pregnant, they could make a lot of money and become popular for being on TV. However, the decrease in the number of teen pregnancies since the shows have aired seems to say otherwise. In fact, many girls are now able to see firsthand how hard it is to raise a baby while in high school. They say that watching these shows has made them decide to practice safe sex or not have sex at all until they are older. Many of the teen moms featured on the shows speak out against getting pregnant at a young age as well.

Amber Portwood, shown here, is one of the stars of MTV's 16 and Pregnant *and* Teen Mom OG.

recorded for U.S. teens in the 65 years for which consistent data are available."[7] In fact, "in 2011, the teen birth rate in the United States fell to the lowest level recorded in nearly 70 years of tracking teen childbearing."[8]

Statistics such as these challenge claims that American teenagers are more sexually active now than in the past. According to sociologist and criminal justice professor Kathleen A. Bogle, the public's alarm over teen sexuality and its ties to pregnancy rates may be uncalled for, at least for older teens: "The virginity rate in college is higher than you think and the number of [sexual] partners is lower than you think ... But so many people think we're morally in trouble, in a downward spiral and teens are out of control. It's very difficult to convince people otherwise."[9] The overall downward trend in the teen pregnancy rate in America since the 1980s indicates that the United States may not be facing a growing moral crisis of teenage sexuality after all.

What About Teens in Other Countries?

Even though the pregnancy rate among teenagers has reached historic lows within the United States in the past decade, American teens are nevertheless far more likely to get pregnant than teenage girls in most other Western industrialized nations that have a similar standard of living to the United States. Despite having declined, the U.S. teen pregnancy rate continues to be one of the highest in the developed world. The rates are lower everywhere in Europe, as well as in Japan and Korea. The high proportion of pregnancies that occur among American teens every year compared with most other countries with similarly advanced economies and standards of living could suggest that American children are learning about sex not only too early, but also in the wrong ways. Many people have criticized American schools' sexual education programs for not providing students with enough information about sex to prevent sexually transmitted diseases (STDs) and unwanted pregnancies.

Teenagers in the United States are having sex earlier in life than their peers in other developed countries, too,

Japan has one of the lowest rates of teen pregnancy in the world.

according to statistics on the number of sexually active American teenagers and the age at which they first had sex. Between 2011 and 2013, among unmarried 15- to 19-year-olds, 44 percent of females and 49 percent of males had had sexual intercourse, and the Guttmacher Institute

MORE TO BE DONE

"The long-term decline in teen pregnancy rates in many countries is great news. Yet it is clear that far more needs to be done to bring down the comparatively high rates in countries like the United States and England and Wales so that they are on par with those in countries like Switzerland and the Netherlands."
—Gilda Sedgh, principal research scientist for the Guttmacher Institute

Rebecca Wind, "Teen Pregnancy Rates Declined In Many Countries Between The Mid-1990s and 2011," Guttmacher Institute, January 23, 2015. www.guttmacher.org/news-release/2015/teen-pregnancy-rates-declined-many-countries-between-mid-1990s-and-2011.

reported that about 70 percent of American teenagers have had sex at least once by the time they are 19. The average age at which teenagers become sexually active in the United States is 17—about a year younger than sexually active teens in Sweden, France, Canada, and Great Britain. Not only are American teens sexually active at earlier ages than teens in many other developed countries, they also tend to have more sexual partners. According to the Guttmacher Institute, "American teenagers who had intercourse in the past year are more likely to have had more than one partner than young people in the other countries, especially those in France and Canada."[10]

The fact that so many more teenage pregnancies occur in the United States than in other developed countries every year could imply that American culture does not adequately educate teens about sex and its possible outcomes, especially pregnancy. Valerie Huber of the National

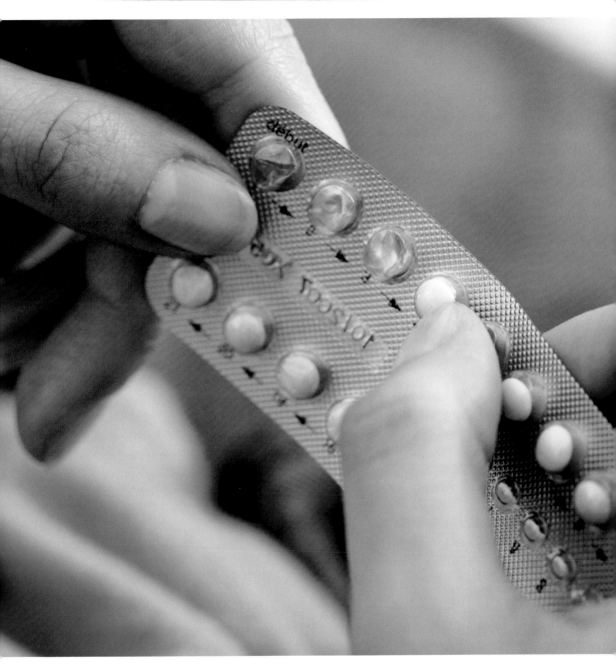

Many believe that different laws about contraception and attitudes toward sex in other countries help to explain the lower rates of teen pregnancy in Europe and Asia.

Abstinence Education Association said, "Contributors [to the rise in teen pregnancy] include an over-sexualized culture, lack of involved and positive role models, and the dominant message that teen sex is expected and without consequences."[11] When America's high teen pregnancy rate is compared with other countries, loose morals again receive much of the blame. When "asked to identify the most serious problem confronting youth, American adults answered that it is the failure of adolescents to learn moral values,"[12] child psychologists Daniel Hart and Gustavo Carlo wrote.

Some people believe if American society adopted more restrictive values and beliefs about sex, marriage, and family, teen sexuality and teen pregnancy rates would drop closer to the rates of other developed countries. Nevertheless, even though U.S. teenagers begin having sex at younger ages and have higher pregnancy rates than teens in other similarly developed countries around the world, research by the Guttmacher Institute shows that by the time they are 19 years old, just as many teens are sexually active in other countries as in the United States. According to social health experts Andrew L. Cherry, Mary E. Dillon, and Douglas Rugh, it is not true that teenagers in America have more interest in sex than teenagers in other countries. "In most of the world, the majority of young women become sexually active during their teenage years," they reported. "A majority of women and men become sexually active by age 20—in developed and developing countries alike."[13] What differs most between the United States and countries with lower teen pregnancy rates is not necessarily teen interest in sex, but the public's opinion that teen sexuality is morally wrong. "Countries other than the United States have attitudes more accepting of adolescent sexual behavior,"[14] the Guttmacher Institute reported. Adult Americans, in contrast, tend to look down on teen sex.

Negative Opinions of Sex Before Marriage

American adults who disapprove of teenage sex may see it as irresponsible behavior that has caused the rates of teen

Planned Parenthood

The Planned Parenthood Federation of America—often called Planned Parenthood—is a nonprofit organization that aims to provide universal access to health care and educate communities about sexual health, including how to prevent pregnancy and the spread of STDs. It operates health clinics where women can be tested for pregnancy, get birth control, have an abortion, or learn about adoption and parenting. Additionally, both men and women can be tested and treated for STDs at the clinics. People who make less than a certain amount of income may qualify to get these services for free, and the organization protects patients' privacy, so teens who are getting an abortion or STD test may not have to tell their parents about it.

Many people who oppose abortion also oppose Planned Parenthood, even though the organization offers other services, too. These opponents do not want the government to help pay for Planned Parenthood's services, which would make them less affordable for low-income women and teens. A woman may also have to walk past protestors who wait outside clinics to tell the women going in that abortion is wrong. For someone who is considering abortion, this can make an already difficult decision even harder.

Some of these opponents have opened crisis pregnancy centers that claim to provide the same services as Planned Parenthood. However, Planned Parenthood warns on its website that "these centers may try to frighten you with misleading films and pictures to keep you from choosing abortion, may lie to you about the medical and emotional effects of abortion, may discourage you from using certain methods of birth control that are very safe and effective,"[1] and more. Planned Parenthood advises making sure the clinic is legitimate before scheduling an appointment.

1. "Crisis Pregnancy Centers," Planned Parenthood, 2016. www.plannedparenthood.org/learn/pregnancy/crisis-pregnancy-centers.

pregnancy in the United States to soar in the past few decades. However, just as there is little difference in the sexuality of 19-year-olds across international borders, there has also been little change in the sexuality of American teens since the 1950s. Contrary to widely held beliefs about uncontrolled teen sex in modern America, the teen pregnancy rate in the United States is not higher than it was generations ago. In fact, American teenagers are actually less likely to have babies now than in previous decades, suggesting that teens were at least as sexually active back then as are modern teens. According to the Pew Research Center, the teen birth rate was almost 50 percent higher in 1957 than it currently is. During the 1950s, though, teen pregnancy did not raise concerns over society's values, and the sexual activity of American teens was not routinely compared with other countries. Author and public speaker Frederica Mathewes-Green explained, "Teen pregnancy is not the problem ... 'Unwed' teen pregnancy is the problem. It's childbearing outside marriage that causes all the trouble."[15]

The average age of marriage in the United States is 25 for women and 27 for men. This average is several years higher than it was in the 1950s, when teenagers who were pregnant before age 20 were far more likely to be married than pregnant teens in America today. Although the age of marriage has risen quite a bit in the past few decades, many Americans' ideas about family values and sexual morals have not changed much. The result is that many teens are having sex, as they have throughout history and as they do almost everywhere around the world, but most of American society still believes that pregnancy ideally should be put off until marriage. Since most teens are not getting married, there is a widespread opinion that they should not be having sex.

In contrast, European countries tend to have more open attitudes about teen sexuality and sex outside of marriage. This difference in attitudes toward teen sexuality can be seen in European sexual education programs. "[Sensible], straightforward sexuality education has reduced teen pregnancy ... in Western Europe," Cherry,

Dillon, and Rugh wrote. "Due in part to public and political resistance to such measures, the United States lags behind other developed countries in the extent to which teenage fertility has declined."[16]

In the four developed countries with which the Guttmacher Institute compared the United States in the

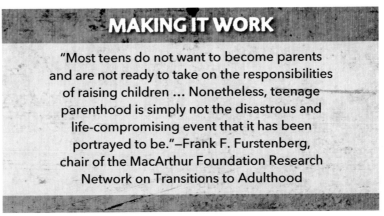

MAKING IT WORK

"Most teens do not want to become parents and are not ready to take on the responsibilities of raising children ... Nonetheless, teenage parenthood is simply not the disastrous and life-compromising event that it has been portrayed to be."—Frank F. Furstenberg, chair of the MacArthur Foundation Research Network on Transitions to Adulthood

Frank F. Furstenberg, *Destinies of the Disadvantaged: The Politics of Teenage Childbearing*, New York, NY: Russell Sage Foundation, 2007, p. 161.

early 2000s, there is general acceptance of teen sexuality as long as it happens within a committed, mature relationship. However, in the United States, teens are more likely to get the message that teenage sex is wrong altogether because they are still too young to be married. "While adults in the other study countries focus chiefly on the quality of young people's relationships and the exercise of personal responsibility within those relationships," the Guttmacher Institute reported, "adults in the United States are often more concerned about whether young people are having sex. Close relationships are viewed as worrisome because they may lead to intercourse."[17]

Teens in Western countries with lower teen pregnancy rates than the United States tend to receive more information about and support for birth control and safe-sex practices than American teens. In the United States, teenagers are often advised to avoid sex completely, and information

Support from friends and family can improve a pregnant teen's view of her situation.

about and access to birth control are not always consistent or easy to find. Marriage, family, and sex therapist Marty Klein wrote, "What a humiliating contrast to Europe and Canada, whose teens have intercourse at roughly the same rate as Americans, but whose national policies on sex education and health have been dramatically more successful in curtailing [decreasing] teen pregnancy."[18] Susie Wilson, founder of the teen sexuality website Sex, Etc. said, "In Europe, their whole society says: 'We're going to teach you … we're not going to punish you.' If you talked to European teens, they have a much more healthy aspect about sex."[19] The high teen pregnancy rate in the United States may result not from poor values and morals, but from a society that fails to accept and support its sexually active—and generally unmarried—teenagers.

Attitudes Toward Children and Teens

Yet another possible explanation for the high rate of teen pregnancy in the United States versus similarly developed countries is that American society's values are perhaps more child-friendly altogether. Society should not assume that all teenage pregnancies are accidental and unwanted. According to the Guttmacher Institute, "Teenage women in the United States are more likely than their peers in other countries to want to become mothers."[20] One study reported that between 2006 and 2010, most teen girls reported that they would be very upset (57.5 percent) or a little upset (29.1 percent) if they got pregnant, while the remaining 13.4 percent of those surveyed said they would be a little or very pleased.[21]

These statistics could mean that American culture is simply fonder of pregnancy and babies than cultures in other countries. Overall, having babies is typically considered a very positive life event in America. "Americans are just generally more optimistic and child-friendly than many countries,"[22] *TIME* magazine reporter Nancy Gibbs wrote. Population, family, and reproductive health professor Nan Marie Astone agreed: "Americans like children. We are the only people who respond to prosperity by saying, 'Let's have another kid.'"[23] In fact, during one of America's greatest times of prosperity, the 1950s, the birth rate skyrocketed to a high of 122 births per 1000 women.[24] It is possible that some teenagers who become pregnant are caught up in America's love of babies and children. The high teen pregnancy rate in the United States might ultimately reflect a culture that prizes children and family, not a culture where family values are in decline.

The teen pregnancy rate does not necessarily reflect a culture of impulsive and irresponsible teenagers, either. "We're convinced that young people are simply incapable of adult responsibility," Mathewes-Green wrote. "We expect that they will have poor control of their impulses, be self-centered and emotional, and be incapable of visualizing consequences." She said these low expectations of teenagers are a fairly recent development. "It wasn't always that way; through much of history, teen marriage and childbearing was the norm."[25] American society may give too little credit to its teenagers and their ability to behave as responsible adults. These low expectations might contribute to the perception that teenagers are incapable of coping maturely with sexual relationships and their consequences. Thus, teen pregnancy may be perceived as a bigger problem than it would be if society generally believed teens could be mature and responsible parents.

Differing Opinions Remain

Despite strong and differing opinions about teen pregnancy, its causes, and what it means for modern American society, it is a situation Americans must continue to study. Teen pregnancy sparks debate in many areas of society, including public health and public education. Responding to the issue will likely require a widespread and unbiased approach. Experts agree that "if we are truly concerned about the welfare of babies, children and adolescents, we must move beyond the moral panic and denial that so often distort the [teen pregnancy] discussion."[26] Although highly controversial, teen pregnancy is not something that Americans can readily ignore. "Every culture has to deal with the sexuality of its young people,"[27] Klein said.

CHAPTER 2

The Far-Reaching Effects of Teen Pregnancy

Some problems are so large that they affect not only the individual involved, but possibly the community, nation, or even the world as well. These issues are known as public health problems, and they are defined as health issues with a negative effect. Because of the number of people these problems affect, it is important for our society to address these problems so their negative consequences can be reduced. The public health field confronts global health issues, such as improving access to health care, controlling infectious diseases, and reducing environmental hazards, violence, substance abuse, and injury. It covers many areas of study and is regularly spotlighted in popular culture and media. Public health professionals must identify which public health problems are the most common, the most dangerous, and the most costly in order to try to limit the harmful effects that these problems have on our society. Some ways to do this can be through educational programs, research, availability of health care, and treatment of affected individuals or groups.

In order for an issue to be classified as a public health problem, a disease or health condition must occur or have the potential to occur among many people. It must also pose significant risks to people's health or the well-being of society, and it must cost society a significant amount of money. Once an issue has been classified as a public health problem, it is up to the professionals to create a course of action to try to solve the problem and stop its effects from becoming more widespread. This can be a time-consuming and expensive process, and many people disagree about the way public health problems are handled within the United States. The controversial issue of teen pregnancy and whether or not it is a public health problem has been discussed and debated for years. People disagree on its classification and on what the response should be in terms of controlling it.

Pregnancy and its Health Risks

Common health risks and dangers of pregnancy can be more serious for a teenager than for an adult woman due to the teenager's younger age and the fact that she still may be developing physically. Adolescents have a higher risk of certain pregnancy-related health problems than adult women do. The bodies of teenagers, especially those younger than age 16, may not be physically prepared for the pregnancy process. Although every woman should regularly see a doctor throughout her pregnancy, Harvard Medical School pediatric professor Joanne E. Cox advised that "adolescents, because of increased maternal and fetal risks, require special prenatal management … Prenatal care is a major factor predicting a positive outcome for a teen birth."[28] The CDC, however, reports that pregnant teenagers are about 35 percent less likely than adult women to seek health care regularly from the start of their pregnancy. According to the CDC, young women in their teens are by far the least likely to receive timely prenatal care. In 2014, young women received prenatal care either late in their pregnancies or not at all—around 25 percent of births to girls under age 15 and 10 percent of births to girls ages 15 to 19 were to those receiving late or no prenatal care. This may be for several reasons: They are ashamed and do not want anyone to know about the pregnancy, they do not have the money to pay for doctor visits, they have no way to get to the doctor's office, or they are unaware of the importance of regular prenatal care. Whatever their reasons, many pregnant teens are reluctant to seek the medical treatment that can help them minimize or manage the possible health risks of pregnancy. This leads some people to consider teen pregnancy a public health problem with potentially serious consequences for teenage girls and their unborn babies.

Malnutrition is a major health risk for pregnant teenagers. A teenage girl's body may still be maturing, especially if she is younger than 16. If she becomes pregnant, some of the nutrients her body needs for its own development may be shifted to her baby instead, which may leave her undernourished and possibly unhealthy. Not all pregnant teenagers become malnourished; those who eat a balanced diet, gain the amount of weight that is healthy for a pregnant woman, and take recommended nutrition supplements are very likely to stay nutritionally healthy during and after pregnancy. However, for teens who are used to unhealthy diets, poor nutrition often continues into pregnancy. If pregnant teens do not seek health care early in their pregnan-

Teens are less likely to seek medical care while pregnant.

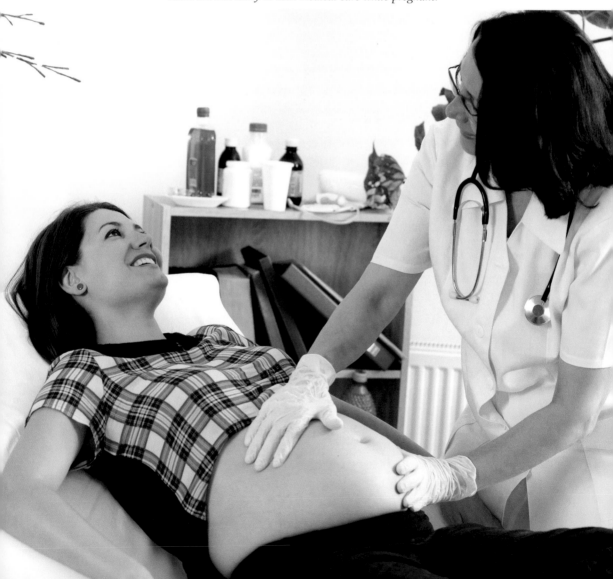

cies, they may remain unaware of the importance of good nutrition for the health of themselves and their babies. Others, wanting to avoid weight gain during pregnancy or not wanting their pregnancy to be obvious to anyone, may even try to diet so they stay thin. Pediatric nursing specialist Nancy T. Hatfield wrote, "Because body image is extremely important to the adolescent, she may use behaviors associated with eating disorders, such as

CHOOSING TO GET PREGNANT

"Pregnancy [is] sometimes viewed as a means of escape: escape from having to go to school, from the community, or from an unhappy home."–Linda Archibald, teen pregnancy researcher and policy consultant

Linda Archibald, "Teenage Pregnancy in Inuit Communities: Issues and Perspectives," Pauktuutit Inuit Women's Association, April 2004. pauktuutit.ca/wp-content/blogs.dir/1/assets/TeenPregnancy_e.pdf.

purging [forced vomiting after meals] or self-starvation, to avoid weight gain during the pregnancy."[29] In the process, these teens could be denying themselves important nutrients and risking nutrition problems such as anemia, which is an iron deficiency that is common during pregnancy and often leads to exhaustion, shortness of breath, and other issues. Without a visit to a health care professional during this time, teens may be unaware of how to care for themselves while they are pregnant.

Pregnant teenagers are also at greater risk than women in their 20s and 30s of developing anemia—low levels of red blood cells—or preeclampsia. Preeclampsia is a condition that causes dangerously high blood pressure during pregnancy and can result in swelling of the hands, legs, and feet. If it is not treated, a severe case can cause seizures, a coma, and possibly even death of the mother, her unborn child, or both. Preeclampsia can occur in any pregnant woman, but it is most common among teenagers and women older than age 40, especially if it is a woman's first pregnancy. Preeclampsia generally can be controlled with proper medical care, but pregnant teenagers who do not get

Depression can be a dangerous side effect of pregnancy, especially for teens.

regular checkups during pregnancy may be unaware of the signs and symptoms of preeclampsia; therefore, they may be at greater risk for serious problems if they develop it.

Depression is another pregnancy-related health problem that tends to be worse among teens. This serious medical condition is marked by severe, constant, long-lasting, and overwhelming feelings of sadness and hopelessness. Women of any age can experience depression during or soon after pregnancy, often because pregnancy-related hormone changes affect their moods. Depression is also common among teenagers in general and is a result of hormone changes and emotional struggles during puberty and adolescence. This issue can have negative health effects on both the mother and her baby. A study from the *Journal of Pediatric and Adolescent Gynecology* suggested that "compared to nonpregnant teens and adults, pregnant teens may have an increased risk for depression."[30] The study also found that the babies of depressed teens were more likely to weigh less when they were born. A low birth weight can have negative health consequences for an infant. Depression is a serious health problem that can have major effects on a person's quality of life and motivation to do things such as work or study. It can even lead to attempts at self-harm or suicide, which makes it a potentially life-threatening complication of pregnancy. The increased risk of depression in pregnant adolescents is another reason why teen pregnancy could be considered a public health problem.

An Already Risky Endeavor Made Riskier

Teens also may be at greater risk of serious injury and even death during childbirth than physically mature women in their 20s and 30s. Giving birth can be dangerous for any woman, regardless of her age. The birth process sometimes results in emergencies such as hemorrhaging (extremely heavy and often fatal bleeding), a breech birth (in which the fetus is turned in such a way that it cannot pass through the birth canal), or a life-threatening infection. Overall, death during childbirth is rare in the United States, where about 17 women in every 100,000 who give birth do not survive, according to the CDC.

However, pregnant girls ages 17 and younger are twice as likely to die while giving birth than mothers who are older than 17. According to pediatrician Jonathan D. Klein, "These risks may be greatest for the youngest teenagers."[31] Around the world, when developing and underdeveloped countries are taken into account, childbirth is actually the leading cause of death among girls ages 15 to 19. This statistic suggests that pregnancy itself poses a real danger to teenagers, especially where proper medical care is not available. Steven Maddocks wrote, "The health risks of teenage pregnancy are very high—in many cases, the girl's body is not yet ready to give birth."[32]

Dangers to the Unborn Child

The possible health risks that a teenage mother faces during pregnancy are only half of the problem. Pregnancy during the teenage years not only puts added strain on a young woman's body, but also often results in health problems for the unborn child. One of the most widespread and potentially harmful problems is preterm labor and delivery, which happens when the mother goes into labor too early (3 weeks or more before the end of the standard 40-week term). Babies born before the 37th week of pregnancy are called premature, and they are more likely to have various health problems than babies who are born at or near the end of the pregnancy term. These problems include brain damage and difficulty with breathing and digestion. According to the World Health Organization, an estimated 15 million babies worldwide—more than 1 in 10—are born too early every year. Among teenage mothers, the premature birth rate is higher. The health effects of being born too early are so serious that many experts see premature birth itself as an issue of public health. Public health professor Barbara Luke wrote, "Prematurity, birth before 37 completed weeks' gestation, is one of the greatest public health problems in the United States today ... Premature babies—preemies—are more than merely small. They are developmentally unprepared for life outside the uterus." Luke added that "children who were born premature are more likely to have respiratory problems during

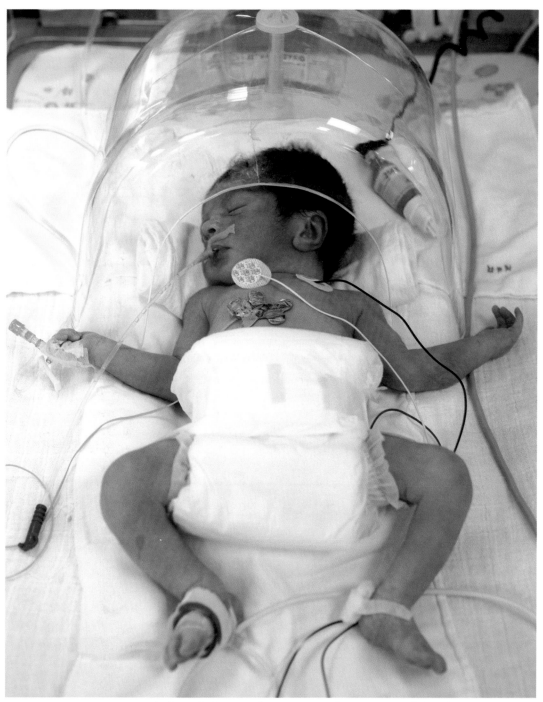

Teens are at a higher risk for giving birth prematurely. A premature baby often faces health problems.

childhood, as well as a higher incidence of learning disabilities and problems with speech, hearing, and vision"[33] later in life. Globally, prematurity is the leading cause of death in children under the age of five.

Another potentially serious problem that commonly affects babies born to teen mothers is low birth weight. Babies who weigh 5.5 pounds (2.5 kg) or less at birth have a high risk for many health problems during infancy and even into childhood and adult life. As infants, low-birth-weight babies are at greater risk for problems such as asthma and other breathing

Dollars and Cents

Teenage pregnancy is not only expensive for the teen and her family, but it also costs the U.S. government and taxpayers billions of dollars in welfare—money the government gives to low-income individuals and families to help provide for their needs—every year. According to the CDC, "In 2010, teen pregnancy and childbirth accounted for at least $9.4 billion in costs to U.S. taxpayers for increased health care and foster care, increased incarceration [imprisonment] rates among children of teen parents, and lost tax revenue because of lower educational attainment and income among teen mothers."[1] This is not something many teens think about when they find out they are pregnant, but it is a very real problem that people often point to in order to prove that teen pregnancy should be classified as a public health problem. Young mothers are more likely to receive help from a program called Temporary Assistance for Needy Families (TANF). This program distributes money from the government to states, and then states use it to help families with children. This is one of the major sources of welfare funding in the United States, and the money to fund TANF comes from taxpayers. The program is controversial; some people approve of it, while others believe tax money should not be used to support teen mothers.

1. "About Teen Pregnancy," Centers for Disease Control and Prevention, April 26, 2016. www.cdc.gov/teenpregnancy/about/.

difficulties, as well as heart and brain defects that occur because their small bodies had not developed fully before birth. When they grow into adults, low-birth-weight babies have as much as 10 times the risk of developing high blood pressure, diabetes, and heart disease. Premature babies are more likely to have a low birth weight than babies born after at least 37 weeks of pregnancy, but about 1 in 10 pregnant teenagers who give birth have a baby with a low birth weight, even if the baby is not born prematurely. The younger a teenage mother is during her pregnancy, the more likely she is to give birth to a low-birth-weight baby. This may occur either because her own body is still developing and competing with the baby for important nutrients or because she did not take good care of herself during pregnancy. According to adolescent health instructors Jeffrey Roth, Jo Hendrickson, Max Schilling, and Daniel W. Stowell, "What female adolescents do to and with their bodies is a causative factor in the higher incidence of low birth weight babies. Some pregnant teens resist medical advice ... concerned with their body image and testing social boundaries, some teens fail to eat properly."[34] Because of the high incidence of low-birth-weight babies among teens—and the serious and costly health problems that persist as these children grow into adulthood—many observers believe teen pregnancy should be classified as a public health problem.

Meeting the Criteria of a Public Health Problem

Teen pregnancy meets the major criteria of a public health problem: It is widespread, occurring among hundreds of thousands of teens each year, and it affects the health, safety, well-being, and productivity of many teens and their infants in negative ways. The health risks of being pregnant at a young age—risks that are not as common in older pregnant women—are also costly to society. They put a potential burden on the doctors and hospitals that treat pregnant teens and provide continued care for newborn children who have long-term health conditions. Because many teens do not finish high

JUST SAY NO?

"There are cultural norms and pressures in this society that make it hard for teens to just say no [to sex], particularly if they lack opportunities to say yes to something else." –Deborah Rhode, Stanford University law professor

Quoted in *Stanford University News Service*, "Teen Pregnancy: Economics More Important than Age," October 20, 1993. www.stanford.edu/dept/news/pr/93/931020Arc3093.html

school before they have a child, they are less likely than high school graduates to have a job that pays enough to support a family. According to Child Trends, "Even after accounting for the fact that teen mothers tend to be from disadvantaged backgrounds, teen parenthood is linked to greater welfare dependence."[35] For some pregnant teenagers, both during pregnancy and after the birth, welfare dependency includes expensive medical bills, which supports the argument that teen pregnancy is an issue with negative effects not only on individual patients, but also on society as a whole. Professor Nweze Eunice Nnakwe wrote, "The personal and societal impact of teenage pregnancy in the United States is huge … Teenage pregnancy is a major public health problem."[36]

There are ways American society might be able to reduce or prevent the health risks associated with teen pregnancy, which is another important factor in the definition of a public health problem. However, Kathleen Sylvester, vice president of a national research and education organization called the Progressive Policy Institute, said "it has been more convenient to declare preventing teen pregnancy 'beyond the capacity of government' than to take an unequivocal moral position against it and take steps to reverse the trend." Sylvester has said more can and should be done to address teen pregnancy as a preventable public health problem: "We must … acknowledge our urgent and compelling national interest in preventing pregnancies by

Educating teens about sex and its consequences is an important component of the campaign to prevent teen pregnancy.

young women unprepared to be mothers."[37] Just as there are public campaigns such as Stamp Out Smoking to teach people about the health-related dangers of cigarettes, public policies could also be developed to educate teenagers about the health risks of pregnancy before age 20. "Progress in reducing teen pregnancy and childbearing will not only improve the well-being of children, families, and communities, but will also reduce the burden on taxpayers,"[38] the National Campaign to Prevent Teen and Unplanned Pregnancy reported. Classifying teen pregnancy as a public health problem might give organizations the public support they require in their efforts to address teen pregnancy.

Falling Short of the Criteria

Pregnancy among teenagers is associated with added health risks to the mothers and their children, but some Americans argue that the true impact of teen pregnancy on the health of society may be overestimated. Although pregnant teenagers do have a higher risk for some pregnancy-related health problems, especially if they are younger than 16, the majority of teen pregnancies (about 73 percent) in the United States occur among teens who are 18 or 19 years old. Women in this older teenage group actually have a lower rate of health problems overall—and, in fact, may even be healthier during pregnancy—than other age groups, particularly women older than age 35. For example, when compared with mothers older than 35, pregnant teens have about half the risk of requiring an expensive emergency procedure called a Caesarean section, in which the baby is surgically removed from the uterus, rather than pushed out through the birth canal. Pregnant women who are 35 or older also have about 14 times the risk of giving birth to a baby with Down syndrome, which is a condition that can cause heart defects and other long-term medical problems, than mothers who are teenagers. Additionally, pregnant women older than 35 have similar (and often even higher) risks of pregnancy complications such as preeclampsia, giving birth prematurely, and having a baby with a low birth weight.

Public opinion is divided on whether or not teen pregnancy should be considered a public health issue.

Teen pregnancy is often debated as a public health problem, but pregnancy over age 35, which carries at least as many health risks, is not. People's concern over the "problem" of teen pregnancy may have more to do with the economic and social position of teens in society than with the actual health risks of teen pregnancy. Debbie A. Lawlor and Mary Shaw of the Department of Social Medicine at the University of Bristol in the United Kingdom argue that the problem is not a medical one, but a social one: "If society were such that a 16-year-old could begin her family at that age, and then say in her mid-20s, return to education or a chosen career path, without prejudice and undue uphill struggle, there would be no problem."[39]

Teen pregnancy and any associated health complications also might not be as widespread as they seem at first glance. Although approximately 750,000 girls and young women under age 20 get pregnant each year, according to the Guttmacher Institute, 60 percent of pregnancies among 15- to 19-year-olds in 2011 ended in birth, while 26 percent ended in abortion and the rest in miscarriage (when a pregnancy is terminated due to natural causes). In 2011, young women ages 19 or younger had 334,000 births and were therefore at risk of health complications related to full-term pregnancy and birth. Compared with widespread health problems such as cancer (affecting 14 million Americans), diabetes (affecting 29 million Americans), or heart disease (affecting 81 million Americans), many experts do not consider teen pregnancy and its health risks to constitute a major public health issue. Children's public health researcher Lisa Arai observed, "The scale of teenage pregnancy and childbearing is often overestimated."[40]

Calling teen pregnancy a health problem, some researchers say, might generate excessive public concern and could actually make the situation worse. "We do not believe that labeling a woman who chooses to have a baby under the age of twenty as a public health problem actually helps the mother or her child," Lawlor and Shaw argued. "We believe that the underlying problem lies in society's attitudes towards young people and specifically in attitudes towards women's reproductive lives."[41] Classifying teen pregnancy as a public health problem implies

The Tragedy of Neonaticide

In 1997, a New Jersey high school student gave birth in the bathroom during her senior prom, disposed of her infant in the bathroom garbage can, and then went back to the dance. Such stories of neonaticide—the killing of a newborn within the first few hours of life—horrify the public. Because those who commit this crime are generally unwed teenagers or women in their early 20s, neonaticide has been used to portray pregnant teens as potentially cruel and unfit for motherhood. However, studies have shown that young women who commit neonaticide are rarely criminally minded. Instead, most are traumatized about pregnancy to the extent that they may be in denial of it. Psychiatrist Laura J. Miller wrote, "For many women, pregnancy raises fears of interpersonal abandonment ... For example, some adolescents who denied their pregnancies had been told they would be kicked out of the house if they became pregnant."[1] When she gives birth, often all alone, a teen who is in denial may panic at the reality of the baby and harm or abandon it without thinking of consequences. Neonaticide accounts for a small percentage of all homicides, but it highlights many controversial issues about teen pregnancy, its contributing factors, and its sometimes drastic consequences.

1. Quoted in Margaret G. Spinelli, ed., *Infanticide: Psychosocial and Legal Perspectives on Mothers Who Kill.* Washington, DC: American Psychiatric Publishing, 2003, p. 11.

that pregnant teenagers and their babies will have health problems and that becoming pregnant as a teenager is an unhealthy event, which is not true for everyone. The health-related issues of teen pregnancy are also tied to many social factors, such as age, race, and socioeconomic status, all of which may affect the health outcome of a teen pregnancy. For this reason, not only does teen pregnancy have a place in national debates over public health, but it has become widely discussed as a social problem in the United States as well.

CHAPTER 3

Teen Pregnancy and Society

Just as there is controversy over whether teen pregnancy qualifies as a public health issue, people also debate whether teen pregnancy is a social problem. A social problem is an issue that threatens the well-being of society. In order to be considered a social problem, members of a community must be concerned about the issue because it may create undesirable results for the future. Social problems can be fixed or solved if community members work together toward a solution, but people must be able and willing to work for that change in order to make it happen. The debate about teen pregnancy being a social issue revolves around whether or not it truly threatens the well-being of society.

Teen pregnancy has been a widespread issue for decades. As a society, we are almost used to hearing statistics about the number of teenagers having babies, and it seems that most people know someone who was a teenage mother. These widespread stories tend to make us believe that teenage pregnancy is a widespread and troubling issue. Another factor contributing to this belief is that teen pregnancy is viewed as a negative experience, and discussion is generally centered on the cost for the parent, the limited opportunities for the child, and the major life adjustment for everyone involved in the situation. To people who have come to think of teen pregnancy as a dire social problem, "it is as if pregnant and parenting teenagers represent all the bad things in society."[42]

Why Teenage Pregnancy May Be Considered a Social Problem

The reasons for considering teen pregnancy to be a social problem are often linked to money. Teenage parents, and especially teenage mothers, generally face steeper economic challenges in life than their peers who put off parenthood, in part because waiting to have children makes it easier for a young woman to attend college or at least finish high school so she can find a job

Pregnancy can make it difficult for teens to finish high school. However, a GED, which is accepted by many colleges and employers as the equivalent to a high school diploma, can be earned by taking an exam.

that pays well. Getting pregnant as a teen, especially for those who choose to give birth and keep their babies, significantly lowers the chances that a young woman will pursue higher education in her lifetime. Although the Guttmacher Institute reported that increasing numbers of pregnant teens and teen mothers are using GED programs to get the equivalent of a high school diploma, about 40 percent of teens who become pregnant never finish high school, compared with only 7 percent of the general population. Only 2 percent of teen mothers receive a college degree by the time they are 30, compared with about 31 percent of the total population.

Bearing and raising children too early in life can make it harder to get a high-paying job to provide for a family because better-paying and stable jobs, especially those with health care benefits for employees and their families, generally go to better-educated adults. People with a bachelor's degree typically earn about 84 percent more than those with only a high school degree. Likewise, much of society views teens who put childbearing before education as problematic because they make life more difficult for themselves and often rely on welfare. Teen mothers have much higher odds of being on welfare at some point in their lives than women who wait until adulthood to have children. About half of all teen mothers apply for public assistance within the first year of having their first child, and 8 in 10 teen mothers will rely on it at some point. These young mothers reflect the gap between what is generally perceived as an ideal situation—people becoming educated and having good jobs before starting families—and what often takes place across America: teenagers having children before they can provide for them.

How Accurate Are the Statistics?

Teen pregnancy may not be quite the drastic and widespread social problem that some make it out to be, however. Despite a slight rise in the teen pregnancy rate between 2005 and 2006, the teen pregnancy rate in the United States has significantly declined overall from what it was in the 1980s and early 1990s. This indicates it is not a problem that is growing uncontrollably. The issue may be exaggerated for political reasons: Teen pregnancy has become a popular topic that helps politicians take a public stand on social values such as family and marriage. According to public policy researchers Alan Cribb and Peter Duncan, "It is partially a 'socially constructed' problem ... Teenage pregnancy symbolizes broader concerns and anxieties about the nature and direction of modern society,"[43] including things such as the perception of declining family values. Despite often being described as a modern concern or one that has gotten worse in recent years, some researchers say that, like many public issues, teen pregnancy just falls in and out of popularity as a social problem, going through periods of intense study and then transforming into something the public ignores. If teen pregnancy is in a period of analysis by the public, however, the attention to it has been intense for years, as magazines, news websites, and TV shows consistently keep the issue in front of the public.

The Media's Influence on Teen Pregnancy

The belief that teen pregnancy has become a social problem of epidemic proportions is often circulated by news outlets. News channels, blogs, and websites frequently report on teen pregnancy trends and may give the American public—particularly American adults, who are the largest audience for news media— the idea that teen pregnancy is both a prevalent social problem and a dangerous one for America's teens. "Most people's perceptions of pregnant and parenting teenagers [are taken] entirely from media sources,"[44] Arai wrote. However, statistics about teenagers who are pregnant may be misunderstood or exaggerated, perhaps to the point of portraying the issue as a major social problem when it may not be one. Arai added, "Journalists covering teenage pregnancy and, through them, their readers, often fail to understand the implications of the [statistics] they are presented with and will readily accept their validity [truth] without proper consideration."[45] The teen pregnancy rates reported in the U.S. media are generally factual, but if the news portrays the number of teen pregnancies as a shocking and troubling fact, then public opinion about teen pregnancy may be swayed. According to educational psychologists Sharon Lynn Nichols and Thomas L. Good, as a result, "the public, whose primary information about all youth sex comes from media accounts of pregnancy or abortion rates, erroneously [wrongly] believes that youth are hormonally driven sexual beings with little self control or responsibility."[46]

THINKING BEFORE ACTING

"In spite of genuine value conflicts among members of communities, it is both possible and crucial to continue encouraging the kind of social conservatism that gives young people pause for thought before becoming sexually active or having sex without protection."
—Naomi Farber, professor of social work, University of South Carolina, Columbia

Naomi Farber, *Adolescent Pregnancy: Policy and Prevention Services.* New York, NY: Springer, 2009, p. 222.

For example, when the media reports a teen pregnancy rate of 750,000 young women every year, the numbers sound shocking. Viewers and readers often conclude that uncontrollable teen promiscuity must be behind such a large number of pregnant teens. The media rarely mention the opposing statistic: More than 90 percent of teenage girls in the United States avoid pregnancy each year. Nichols and Good also pointed out that media statistics of any kind are often misleading: "Statistics tell relatively little about the complicated nature of youth's sexual lives, and although they are useful indicators for gauging youth's sexual activity, they fail to provide accurate accounts of the conditions under which sexual behavior occurs."[47] For instance, Nichols and Good stated that adults often see teen pregnancy rates as proof of oversexed teenage boys and girls; however, in more than half of pregnancies that occur among teens, the father is several years older than the teen mother and is often not a teenager himself. When

Advertisements often contain sexual images or messages.

sex between teenage girls and adult men is considered, Nichols and Good wrote, "we see a strikingly different picture from the common notion that young teens are irresponsibly following hormonal desires with each other."[48] This suggests there may be much more behind the culture of American teenagers and their sexual practices than media statistics show.

Some people believe the media is also partly responsible for promoting teenage sexuality that leads to pregnancy, not just for reporting teen pregnancy trends. "Our vast media culture is replete with explicit and implicit messages about youth sex and its role," Nichols and Good wrote. "Entertainment and advertising saturate the market with sexual content and images of youthful, physical beauty. According to these messages, sex is exciting, healthy, and a powerful determiner of individual worth."[49] It may not be surprising, with the media onslaught of sexual content in the past few decades, that more teenagers might be experimenting with sex. According to pediatric health researcher Rebecca Collins and her colleagues, "TV may create the illusion that sex is more central to daily life than it truly is and may promote sexual initiation as a result ... Teens who see characters having casual sex without experiencing negative consequences will be more likely to adopt the behaviors portrayed."[50] Nichols and Good, however, argued that the media should not necessarily be assumed to be a bad influence on teens and that "there is some evidence that sex in the media helps youth make decisions and sort out complex sexual situations."[51] Seeing teenagers in movies and television programs who are faced with sexual decisions could help real-life teenagers decide what their own beliefs and attitudes are about sex and its consequences.

The Effects of Race and Culture on Teen Pregnancy

Whatever effects the media may have on the public perception of teen pregnancy as a problem, one of the most reported aspects of teen pregnancy has to do with its ties to race. Statistically, women in certain minority groups are more likely than women of other groups to become pregnant before age 20, and teens who are African American or Latina have the highest teen pregnancy rate of all ethnicities in the United States. According to the Guttmacher Institute, approximately 12 percent of African American and Latina teens ages 15 to

Abstinence: A Popular Choice?

Sex in the media is often blamed for having a role in teen pregnancy, and songs with sexually explicit lyrics and music videos have especially been accused of idolizing sexuality and making casual sex seem tempting to teens. Pop singer Lady Gaga is one star who has received negative attention by making music videos and stage appearances while scantily dressed and singing about sexually suggestive topics. However, Lady Gaga has spoken out in support of abstinence, which seems to have become a trend among many other stars as well. Miley Cyrus, Selena Gomez, Carrie Underwood, and Jordin Sparks have all, at one time or another, publicly supported abstinence until marriage. All of the Jonas Brothers took virginity pledges in their teens, although not all of them followed through on those pledges. Even famous athletes, such as NFL quarterback Russell Wilson, have publicly announced their support for abstaining from sex until marriage. Wilson and his wife, singer Ciara, announced that because of Wilson's religious beliefs, they would be abstaining until their wedding day. The verdict is still out, however, on whether the media actually contributes to teen pregnancy, and stars may have less influence—good or bad—than they or the public believe.

Russell Wilson and Ciara were very public about their choice to remain abstinent until they married.

19 become pregnant in the United States each year. This is 3 times higher than the percentage of white teenagers the same age who become pregnant every year. Teenage girls who are Native American have slightly lower rates of pregnancy than African Americans and Latinas but still far higher than the teen pregnancy rate among whites. Such disparities, or inequalities, are sometimes interpreted as evidence of persistent racial inequity in the United States. According to social history professor Linda Gordon, "Teenage and out-of-wedlock pregnancy has become a widely racialized issue" that is affected by "accelerating impoverishment and inequality."[52]

Another explanation for this racial gap may be that while African Americans and Latinas often do not actively want to get pregnant, they may also not be trying to prevent pregnancy by using birth control methods such as condoms. One study among a group of male and female Latinx students found various factors that influenced teens' sexual choices and views of pregnancy. For example,

> *for those with no sexual experience, their mother's education (having at least completed high school ... or having some college education) decreased their PWS [Pregnancy Wantedness Scale] scores. Males ... who considered religion important in their sexual behavior had higher [PWS] scores, suggesting that traditional religious views encourage [wanting a family].*[53]

Although Latina and African American teens are still at a higher risk of pregnancy than white teens, their rates have dropped faster than the overall pregnancy rate. The Pew Charitable Trusts reported that due to the "increased use of highly effective, low maintenance birth control methods like the IUD [intrauterine device] and contraceptive implants"[54] since 1991, the teen birth rate has declined by 67 percent for African Americans, 60 percent for Latinas, and 63 percent for Native Americans. For whites, it only declined 57 percent. However, African American and Latina girls are still twice as likely as whites to become pregnant in their teens.

Although the statistics show that certain racial groups are more at risk than others, the reasons for this are still being

Racial Group	Current teen pregnancy rate (2013)	% Decline since 2012	% Decline since 1991
Non-Hispanic whites	19 births per 1,000	9%	57%
Non-Hispanic blacks	39 births per 1,000	11%	67%
Hispanics	42 births per 1,000	10%	60%
American Indians or Alaska Natives	31 births per 1,000	11%	63%
Asians or Pacific Islanders	9 births per 1,000	10%	68%

The information in this chart was provided by the National Campaign to Prevent Teen and Unplanned Pregnancy.

debated. Because African American and Latinx teens are more likely to grow up in poverty, many people argue that the focus should be on economics rather than race. Teen pregnancy "is an issue across all cultures, across all populations, and, to be frank, it has been a problem forever," retired professor of child development Martha Kello said. "Now, whether or not it is a racial culture that's the issue or whether or not it is

A BIG RESPONSIBILITY

"With the age of puberty decreasing and the age of first marriage increasing, the average American now spends some 10 years being sexually mature and unmarried ... There's never been a generation in human history from whom this many years of abstinence-until-marriage has been expected."–Marty Klein, marriage, family, and sex therapist.

Marty Klein, *America's War on Sex: The Attack on Law, Lust, and Liberty.* Westport, CT: Praeger, 2006, p. 9.

one of economics, religion or education, that happens to be a major question."[55]

Religion's Role in Teen Pregnancy

As Kello pointed out, religion is another cultural factor that has become a significant part of the debate over teen pregnancy. Some people claim that teen pregnancy is a symptom of a society in which religion has become less important; they believe that stricter and more traditional religious values across society could actually reduce teen pregnancy. According to Methodist minister and professor Steven Emery-Wright,

> The level of a young person's religious commitment almost always makes a difference to his/her sexual attitudes and practice ... Young people's faith will also most likely mirror that of their parents. An obvious consequence of this is that children of parents with strong Christian commitments will have a lower incidence of teenage pregnancy.[56]

Stronger religious beliefs throughout the population will not necessarily reduce teen pregnancy, however. Evidence suggests that strict religious beliefs may actually add to the teen pregnancy problem. According to a 2010 survey conducted by the Pew Research Center on religion and public life, in 2009, teen pregnancy rates surged in states such as Mississippi that were rated as having conservative Christian values. The rise in the number of teen pregnancies in states with highly religious populations suggests that teen pregnancy is not necessarily a result of weakened religious values. Sociologist Mark D. Regnerus wrote, "While religion certainly influences the sexual decision making of adolescents, it infrequently motivates the actions of religious youth. In other words, religious teens do not often make sexual decisions for religious reasons."[57] In addition, according to a study conducted for the *Journal of Marriage and the Family*, Marlena Studer and Arland Thornton found that among 18-year-olds, "never-married, sexually experienced ... girls regularly attending religious services were less likely to have used an effective, medical method of contraception than those who were rarely attending religious services."[58] This may be because some religions discourage the use of contraceptives.

Religion, like race, may have a certain effect on teen pregnancy rates, but it is not the sole cause or the sole means of prevention. Pregnancy occurs in teens of all cultures and religious beliefs, so there clearly is more to the issue than just race or religious values.

The Poverty Problem

Some say the common cultural link between teenagers and pregnancy has nothing to do with race or religion, but instead with money. Economics is perhaps the most highly contested factor in the debate over teen pregnancy. On an individual level, poverty and teen pregnancy often occur together in the same populations. Communities that are economically disadvantaged tend to have much higher rates of teen pregnancy than wealthier areas, regardless of the racial, ethnic, or religious makeup of those communities. On a wider scale, teen pregnancy is also related to the economic well-being of the country as a whole because the cost of providing for teen mothers and their babies sometimes falls on taxpayer-funded welfare programs. The U.S. government spends an estimated $7 billion or more every year to provide financial assistance to teenagers who become parents to help them pay for living expenses such as housing and food. According to the National Campaign to Prevent Teen and Unplanned Pregnancy, teenage childbearing also costs taxpayers approximately $9.4 billion each year. This money has become one of the most prominent aspects of the argument as to whether teen pregnancy is a social problem. "Many stereotypes have emerged about 'welfare moms,'" cultural anthropologist Barbara Miller wrote. "These women, some people believe, have babies because they want welfare money."[59] Because a majority of teens who become pregnant are already poor and may see few other economic prospects for their lives, there is concern that the promise of welfare benefits for unwed teen mothers may actually be an incentive for some teens to become pregnant instead of getting a job. However, this myth has been disproven time and time again. The money a mother gets from the government is not enough to support her and a child if she does not also have a job. Additionally, TANF is only given to people who can prove they are actively looking for work or taking classes to improve their situation.

Living in poverty is a strong predictor that a young woman will become pregnant before she is 20, although not because she wants to qualify for welfare. It is estimated that about 60 percent of pregnant teenagers live in poverty when they become pregnant, and about 80 percent of those who give birth and become mothers will live in poverty and require welfare services at some point. Motherhood creates many challenges for a teen, making it less likely that she will ever graduate from high school or attend any kind of postsecondary school. Without these diplomas, a teen mother is less likely than better-educated peers to find a job that pays her enough money to support her family without living in poverty and receiving welfare assistance. Additionally, "adolescent girls who become mothers have fewer options for their future," Cherry, Dillon, and Rugh wrote. "Early childbearing often limits school and job possibilities for these girls, which helps explain why so many of the world's young mothers live in poverty."[60] With or without welfare, pregnancy is often considered an economic trap for teenagers; once they become parents, they may always struggle economically. According to environmental health professor John B. Conway, teen pregnancy "is the single most reliable predictor of welfare dependency in this country."[61]

The statistics may not accurately describe the connection between teen pregnancy and being poor, though. In fact, much debate centers on whether poverty contributes to teen pregnancy or whether teen pregnancy causes poverty. "With disadvantage creating disadvantage," educational psychologist Frank D. Cox wrote, "it is no wonder that teen pregnancy is widely perceived as the very hub of the U.S. poverty cycle."[62] However, those who support eliminating poverty as a way to reduce teen pregnancy in America may be giving poverty too large a role as a cause of teen pregnancy in the first place. "Poverty does not inevitably lead to unwed adolescents' pregnancies," psychoanalyst Anne L. Dean wrote. "Further, the eradication of poverty, if this were possible, would not speedily eliminate the unwed teen-age pregnancy behavior pattern."[63] Even characterizing teen pregnancy as a social problem with ties to poverty might be doing a disservice to pregnant teenagers. "It seems that, at best, teenage pregnancy is something which young women 'drift into' because of otherwise unfulfilled and problem-atic lives," Cribb and Duncan wrote. "Does this mean that it

Teen parents who have financial troubles may be able to get food from their local community soup kitchen.

cannot be seen as a positive choice, as an expression of personal autonomy [independence], as a valid means of becoming fulfilled rather than simply as a barrier to fulfillment?"[64]

There is debate over how much social factors such as poverty cause teen pregnancy, but many researchers say that classifying teen pregnancy as a social problem is unlikely to be helpful. Instead, they recommend that the focus be shifted from labeling teen pregnancy as a problem to finding effective ways for teens to learn about sexuality and its consequences. In this regard, adult discussions about teen pregnancy and its problem status may leave teens with little actual guidance on sexuality and parenthood. Amid the controversy about how much of a health or social problem teen pregnancy is and how it should be addressed, American teens have been placed at the center of another great battle—how best to help them avoid pregnancy, or at least unintended pregnancy, in the first place.

CHAPTER 4

Decreasing the Teen Pregnancy Rate

The topic of teen pregnancy is one that is hotly debated in the United States. Some people argue that it is a pressing public health and social problem, while others say that it is not that big of an issue. However, few people would argue that no effort should be made to reduce teen pregnancy rates. Pregnant teens face increased health risks over their peers who do not become pregnant. They also face many emotional and financial challenges as they attempt to raise their children while they are still completing their schooling. "The vast majority of babies born to single teens remain at home with their young mothers," Charles Zastrow and Karen K. Kirst-Ashman wrote. "This places these young women in a very different situation than that of most of their peers … The additional responsibility of motherhood poses serious restrictions on the amount of freedom and time available"[65] for typical teen pastimes such as socializing, going to school, and making career choices. Pregnant teens are certainly at a disadvantage when it comes to living an average teenage life.

This is not to say that every teen who becomes pregnant will have health problems, struggle financially, or even drop out of school. In fact, many teens complete high school and even attend college, despite the fact that they were pregnant at a young age. A young woman's life is not ruined if she gets pregnant, but it does lead to a number of complications. For these reasons, many Americans believe that teens should wait until they are adults to become pregnant. Many people also believe it is our responsibility as a society to teach teenagers how to prevent pregnancy so they will not run the risk of encountering these complications.

Many people disagree about how old is "old enough" to have children.

However, despite the belief that teenage pregnancy has negative consequences, there is some disagreement over teaching teenagers how to prevent pregnancy. First, the age at which a teenager could be considered an adult who is ready for parenthood is widely debated. For example, 73 percent of all teenage pregnancies occur among women who are 18 or 19 years old; by this age, they are considered legal adults who can lawfully marry. People argue that an 18- or 19-year-old who is married is responsible enough to raise a child. Sociologist Karen Sternheimer said, "We've redefined adolescence as an extension of childhood, whereas it used to be a precursor to adulthood."[66] Many people also argue that if a teenager is old enough to join the military at age 18, then he or she is old enough to raise a child. "We like to infantilize teens, or focus on their bad behavior, even though some of them are functioning as adults,"[67] Sternheimer explained. For these reasons, some argue that a public campaign is not necessary because it does not apply to all teens who are pregnant.

JUST DON'T DO IT

"The only thing my mother told me about sex is not to have it. That's not really an education."
—Anonymous girl, age 17

Quoted in National Campaign to Prevent Teen and Unplanned Pregnancy, *Parent Power: What Parents Need to Know and Do to Help Prevent Teen Pregnancy*. Washington, DC: National Campaign to Prevent Teen and Unplanned Pregnancy, p. 16. www.thenational.campaign.org/resources/pdf/pubs/ParentPwr.pdf.

The issue of whether, and at what age, teen pregnancy should be prevented has largely become a matter of debate over social values. Many people, teens included, believe the teen years, at least prior to high school graduation, are simply too early for any young adult to become a parent. Other people say the real argument is not about teen pregnancy, but instead about whether teen parents are married and whether unwed pregnancies at any age are appropriate. According to Maggie Gallagher, founder of the Institute for Marriage and Public Policy, "What we have called our 'teen pregnancy' crisis is not really about teenagers. Nor is it really about pregnancy ... What has changed most in recent decades is not who gets pregnant, but who gets married."[68] Still other people avoid the controversial topic of marriage altogether and say that American society should focus on preventing unintended pregnancy among all women, especially teenagers. According to a report by the U.S. Department of Health and Human Services, "The consequences of unintended pregnancy are not confined to those occurring in teenagers or unmarried couples ... for teenagers, the problems associated with unintended pregnancy are compounded ... Reducing unintended pregnancies is possible and necessary."[69] However, even if the goal of preventing teen pregnancy is restated as cutting down on the number of unwanted pregnancies among teens, rather than negatively judging teen pregnancy in general, there is still a huge debate among adults and teens alike about the best way to reach that goal.

The Controversy Over Abstinence

Abstinence is the act of avoiding a certain activity as a means of also avoiding negative consequences associated with that activity. In discussions about sex, abstinence means refraining from some or all types of sexual contact with another person. Because abstinence is the only absolute way to avoid pregnancy, many people promote abstinence as the best method of pregnancy prevention that American society can recommend to teenagers. Many teenagers are themselves supportive of abstinence as the one fail-proof way to avoid pregnancy until they are ready. "Abstinence is the only surefire way to avoid getting pregnant," Lynne Collenback said. "It has become a matter of what I believe is right and wrong for myself."[70] Teen abstinence, say its supporters, has the added benefit of preventing the spread of STDs, such as gonorrhea and HIV/AIDS, and it also shifts teenagers' attention from sex and its possible consequences, both physical and emotional, to more potentially beneficial pastimes such as school and extracurricular activities.

During the late 1990s and early 2000s, the administrations of former presidents Bill Clinton and George W. Bush both passed measures that supported a national abstinence education program for America's teens. The policy coincided with changes in the sexual activity and pregnancy patterns of America's teens, including a 10 percent drop from 1995 to 2002 in the number of high school teenagers who had ever had sex and an approximately 38 percent drop in teen pregnancy rates during the same period. Bruce Cook, a spokesperson for a nonprofit group that supports abstinence-focused education, said, "Programs will work that encourage our young people to abstain from at-risk sexual behavior."[71] To supporters of abstinence during the early 2000s, it seemed that more teenagers were remaining abstinent longer and that this was reducing teen pregnancy rates. "The more teens clearly understand the benefits to abstinence until marriage and the risks of premarital sexual behavior, the more they will make the right choices,"[72] Cook said. However, studies have since shown that there were likely other reasons for the decline in pregnancy rates.

The idea of abstinence as a national policy for preventing teen pregnancy in the United States has been criticized in part because those who support abstinence, especially abstinence until marriage, may make certain value judgments. For example, they may claim that sexually active teenagers have made poor moral decisions. Not all Americans believe that marriage is or should be a goal for teenagers; therefore, a philosophy that puts marriage before sex simply does not make sense for some teens. A number of people, adults and teenagers alike, also believe that the expectation for teenagers to remain abstinent until marriage, or at least until adulthood, is unrealistic and even counterproductive. They believe that abstinence programs set teenagers up to feel like they have not succeeded at an important expectation if they do have sex. "We are training a whole generation that 'if' (actually when) they have sex before marriage, that they have failed," Marty Klein wrote. "Almost 90 percent of abstinence pledgers have intercourse before marriage—and they protect themselves and each other at a lower rate than nonpledgers."[73]

As Klein pointed out, those who are taught to practice abstinence only are less likely to use a form of birth control, such as condoms, if they do have sex than teenagers who are taught about alternatives to abstinence. This contributes to evidence that promoting abstinence as the only real way to prevent pregnancy could perhaps result in more teenagers engaging in unprotected sexual relationships that may result in pregnancy. Those who oppose abstinence-only education do not necessarily think the suggestion that "abstinence is best" encourages teenagers to rebel and have sex; rather, they feel that it contributes to teen pregnancy by not giving teenagers information or alternatives to avoid pregnancy if they do have sex. Additionally, some people are concerned about the emotional impact of abstinence-only education. Debra Hauser, vice chair of the American Sexual Health Association's (ASHA) board of directors, believes that this type of program is

> one of our worst enemies because of the overwhelming shame and fear that it attaches to healthy sexual behavior. Abstinence-only education ... teaches sexuality as a dirty and damaging trait that must be controlled ... Once [teens have] matured into adults and find that their sexual urges have not gone away, they will often feel ashamed and confused because of how sex has been stigmatized throughout their adolescence. As a result, their emotional and physical health will be greatly harmed, whether through internalized shame, less willingness to use condoms, and/or lack of awareness about STD testing and pregnancy prevention.[74]

There is no argument that abstinence is the only totally fail-proof method of preventing pregnancy—as long as those who practice it never slip up. Margaret O. Hyde

Some people wear purity rings to show their commitment to abstinence. However, studies have found that abstinence pledges are often broken.

Pregnant in High School

Before 1972, public schools in the United States could forbid pregnant teens from attending classes or participating in extracurricular activities based on the assumption that pregnancy made it impossible for a young woman to do well in school. It was also widely believed that a pregnant classmate would distract other students. In 1972, national legislation called Title IX was passed to eliminate gender-based discrimination in schools. In addition to giving young women equal opportunity to take certain classes, participate in sports, and attend college, Title IX made it illegal for U.S. public schools to treat pregnant students differently than any other students. Pregnant teenagers now have the right to attend school up to the day they give birth, to participate in all sports and extracurricular activities, and to be granted a period of excused absence from school once the baby is born. After Title IX was passed, the school dropout rate for pregnant teenagers declined by one-third. Today, many schools even provide special study programs, such as evening and correspondence classes, to make it easier for teenage mothers to complete their education and improve their opportunities for the future. There are some schools in New York City that are even set up to help pregnant high school students finish their education. These schools, such as the Martha Nielson School in the Bronx, provide parenting classes and daycare, in addition to the regularly offered high school curriculum.

Some schools offer childcare classes for teen moms in addition to regular school subjects.

and Elizabeth H. Forsyth wrote, "While some claim that abstinence is 100 percent safe, this is true only when it is practiced 100 percent of the time."[75] Many people are unconvinced that teenagers, as a population, will be committed enough to abstinence to practice it unfailingly. In fact, some teenagers never plan to remain abstinent, and even many who claim to believe strongly in abstinence become sexually active anyway. Therefore, teaching teenagers how to have sex safely may be preferable to setting up an unrealistic expectation for them not to have sex and then giving them no information about preventing pregnancy if they do become sexually active.

Educating Teens

Supporters of a comprehensive approach to teaching teens about sex state that to really prevent pregnancy, teenagers need factual, scientific information about the sexual process. There are two different types of programs. The first, "abstinence-plus" education, promotes abstinence as the best option, but it also gives information about other forms of contraception, or birth control methods, that are available to teenagers, including prescription birth control pills, injections, and skin patches, all of which release pregnancy-preventing hormones into a woman's body. Most abstinence-plus sex education programs also teach the proper use of condoms, which are important not just to prevent pregnancy, but also to reduce the risk of exchanging STDs. The second type of program, known as comprehensive sex education, not only teaches about contraceptives, but also gives teenagers information about the emotional aspects of sexual relationships, which is a topic not covered in abstinence-only or abstinence-plus programs. Supporters of sex education feel the comprehensive program is the best because, in addition to giving teens important information about how to avoid STDs and pregnancy, it teaches them about their bodies and encourages open communication about sex in relationships. Rather than keeping important information from teens—as abstinence-only programs are often accused of doing—or shaming them into remaining abstinent—a criticism of abstinence-plus programs—supporters of a comprehensive sex education approach are in favor of giving teens access to information they need in order to make decisions about their own sexuality. Adolescent health physician John Santelli said, "Abstinence-only programs are inherently coercive by withholding information needed to make informed choices and promoting questionable and inaccurate opinions."[76]

Supporters of comprehensive sex education claim it is more effective at reducing teen pregnancy than teaching only about abstinence. These supporters believe that if teenagers do become sexually active, they do so with knowledge about how pregnancy occurs and how to prevent it. Many teenagers say they appreciate programs that teach facts about sex objectively and scientifically, rather than programs that moralize and try to shape their sexual behavior or do not give all the facts. Bethany, a 17-year-old girl, said, "Teenagers are not all stupid, but all of us need help ... Don't hold back from 'the talk' or sharing information hoping that it will protect your children, because it only hurts them when they get the wrong information."[77] Many teens feel that knowing accurate information is helpful in preventing pregnancy. The Kaiser Family Foundation, a nonprofit organization that studies health care issues facing the United States, reported that "young people feel great pressure to have sex, with a majority saying that while putting off sex may be a 'nice idea, nobody really does.'"[78] Comprehensive sex education aims to give teenagers enough facts and information to make informed decisions about sex, whether or not they choose to become sexually active.

Supporters of a more conservative approach to sex education, meanwhile, argue that comprehensive and abstinence-plus education may actually give teenagers mixed messages about protecting themselves from pregnancy. Many opponents of abstinence-plus education say such programs teach that abstinence is best but then give detailed

Condoms not only prevent pregnancy, but also the spread of STDs.

information about what to do if teenagers fail to remain abstinent. Comprehensive programs are sometimes criticized for giving teenagers the idea that it is okay, and even expected, that they will become sexually active before adulthood. The conservative coalition Concerned Women for America believes that supporters of abstinence-plus sex education "want to sabotage the authentic abstinence message by including instruction in condom and contraception use." The coalition added, "That's a mixed message. We don't tell children not to do drugs and then give them clean syringes in case they do. We don't tell them not to smoke and then give them low-tar cigarettes because those are the least harmful."[79] Many supporters of abstinence-only education fear that abstinence-plus and comprehensive sex education will lead teens to engage in sexual behavior that puts them at risk for becoming pregnant. For this reason, many parents oppose the practice of schools making condoms available to students. However, Advocates for Youth, an organization that aims to raise awareness among young adults about sexual health, reported that "a study of New York City's school condom availability program found a

TOOLS FOR TRUST

"Give young people the tools and, more and more, they will make safe and responsible decisions. Deprive them of critical information, and we'll continue our dubious track record as the least successful nation in the Western industrialized world in dealing with teens and sexuality."–James Wagoner, former president of Advocates for Youth

James Wagoner, "Teens Need Information, Not Censorship," National Coalition Against Censorship Press Event, June 12, 2001. www.advocatesforyouth.org/index.php? option=com_content&task=view&id=761&Itemid=58.

significant increase in condom use among sexually active students but no increase in sexual activity."[80]

Whereas opponents of abstinence-only education say that teenagers are unlikely to be abstinent 100 percent of the time, opponents of comprehensive sex education similarly argue that birth control methods are highly effective only when used—and used correctly—100 percent of the time. Sexually active teenagers are not this faithful to the use of birth control methods, according to the National Campaign to Prevent Teen and Unplanned Pregnancy; as many as one-third of sexually active teenagers who use some form of birth control do so inconsistently. According to a study by the CDC, 21 percent of teen females and 16 percent of teen males reported they did not use contraception at first intercourse. Although supporters of comprehensive sex education believe this statistic merely means more should be taught to teenagers about the importance of consistently using birth control methods, people who favor abstinence-only education disagree, saying that any sex among teens is exposing them to unnecessary risk of pregnancy. The American College of Pediatricians, for example, stated that it "strongly endorses abstinence-until-marriage sex education and recommends adoption by all school systems in lieu [instead] of 'comprehensive sex education.'" It said "this position is based on the public health principle of primary prevention—risk avoidance in lieu of risk reduction, upholding the 'human right to the highest attainable standard of health.'"[81] In other words, it may not be enough to merely lessen a teen's risk of pregnancy by improving access to and use of birth control. Abstinence supporters say society is obligated to try to eliminate the risk of unwanted pregnancy altogether, and abstinence is the only completely effective way.

The Sex Ed Debate

Abstinence-only, abstinence-plus, and comprehensive sex education supporters all face opposition, not just from people with different beliefs about the best way to teach

America's teenagers about sex and the prevention of pregnancy, but also from people who disagree about where—and whether—such lessons should even be taught. Public schools have become a battleground for the debate on sex education; the vast majority of America's teenagers attend public schools, so these have become the most obvious settings in which to give information to teens about sex and pregnancy. "The many public consequences of sexual activity among teenagers make [sex education] an appropriate subject of public education,"[82] political writer Amy Gutmann wrote. The intense controversy about which sexual information is best is sometimes complicated by communities that question not only which program to use, but also who should decide what gets taught. "Many different types of organizations now play an important role in sexuality education," sex educators Clint Bruess and Jerrold Greenberg reported. "The schools have remained a basic potential source of sexuality education programs, but religious organizations, voluntary agencies, health departments, professional schools, and even clubs now contribute to overall sexuality education efforts."[83] Even if schools, school districts, parents, and other organizations can reach a consensus on the type of program that is best, it is still difficult to narrow down the specific information that will be most useful and the best materials and methods for teaching it. "Today, the problem is often in wading through the many resources to evaluate them and decide which are most useful,"[84] Bruess and Greenberg wrote.

Adding to the controversy over what should be taught with regard to sex education, in many communities parents with differing opinions argue over whether it is a public school's place to teach children about sex. Conservative blogger Lisa H. Warren argued that "schools need to focus on academics and leave teaching about 'the rest of life' or 'personal life' to parents … The government (public school) has no right to attempt to involve itself in matters of morality and sexuality."[85] The sex education curriculum taught in many communities is closely monitored by parents who

Some people think that teaching sex education in schools is not right. They argue that kids should receive sex education at home from their parents.

A Backup Plan

A kind of medication known as emergency contraception is available for women to take after having unprotected sex in order to prevent an unwanted pregnancy. Commonly called the morning-after pill, this medication can actually be used up to three days after unprotected sex, although it is most effective if a woman takes it within 24 hours after having unprotected sex. The medication is a dose of hormones, similar to birth control pills, that prevents the woman's body from releasing an egg or stops a released egg from being fertilized. In some cases, it may also stop the fertilized egg from attaching to the uterus. Although emergency contraception is not a fail-proof method (Depending on how soon after sex it is taken, it can reduce the risk of pregnancy by 52 to 94 percent.), it could prevent unwanted pregnancy among teenagers who have had unprotected sex and regret it immediately afterward.

Some people oppose the pill because of a dispute over when life begins. The medical definition of pregnancy is when the fertilized egg attaches to the uterine wall, but some people believe the pill may actually be killing an already conceived child because they consider the fertilization of the egg to be the moment when life starts. In most cases, the pill prevents the egg from being fertilized at all, so even by the strictest standards of when life begins, no abortion is taking place. The most common brand of emergency contraception is Plan B, which is available without a prescription for women ages 15 and over, although its relatively high cost (from $40 to $50)

may challenge whether the content is appropriate. School districts, not wanting to create controversy among parents, sometimes find themselves forced to restrict or compromise on what they can teach teenagers about sexuality, safe sex, and prevention of teen pregnancy. Some school districts do not teach it at all. Currently, "only 22 states mandate sex education, and only 13 require the information to be may make it hard for teenagers to buy on their own. Another objection to the pill is that its easy availability will encourage promiscuity among teens who think they no longer have to worry about pregnancy. However, studies have shown that this is untrue. In 2013, the New York City Department of Health reported that, while the proportion of sexually active students using Plan B had increased, the proportion of sexually active students overall had decreased.

Now that Plan B is available over the counter, more teens are using it to prevent pregnancy.

'medically accurate.'"[86] Some parents see this as a good thing: "Mandatory sex education is as offensive to parents who believe in the sanctity of sex as mandatory prayer is to parents who do not believe in God," Gutmann wrote. At the same time, she said, "teenagers, not their parents, are required to take sex education courses."[87] Many teenagers, however, say they appreciate the opportunity to learn about things such as pregnancy and its prevention in school. Karen, a high school sophomore in Indiana, said, "Sexual education is a valuable topic ... If we didn't have that class, many of us would have unsafe sex, simply because we don't know how to use contraceptives."[88]

Most Americans agree that teenagers need some sort of guidance from adults if they are to approach sexual situations maturely, responsibly, and in ways that do not lead to unwanted pregnancy. However, harsh disagreements continue over what lessons on sexuality should be taught in public schools. Activist Caitlin Shetter said, "It is a shame that adults and policymakers spend their time arguing over what is better and more effective: abstinence-only sex education or education about contraceptives. While they are arguing, thousands of teens are having sex and getting pregnant."[89]

Furthermore, while formal sex education remains in dispute, teenagers are constantly surrounded by depictions of sex. A primary source of this exposure is the media, and in the absence of consistent sex education in schools, TV and movies could be where teens turn most often to learn about sexuality. About 70 percent of the most popular TV shows among teenagers show sexual content, according to the Kaiser Family Foundation, and 28 percent of teens report getting information about sex from websites. A 2004 study by the Rand Corporation showed that teens who watched the most television with sexual content were twice as likely to have sex within the following year as teens who watched the least. While arguments rage over the issue of sex education, those who may be hurt most are the teens left to get the majority of their knowledge of sex and pregnancy prevention from television. "It is inexcusably lazy to let Hollywood and prime time television stand in for accurate information about sex,"[90] Courtney E. Martin said.

Sex and pregnancy remain constant realities for American teens, despite all the controversies over how best to help teens avoid making sexual decisions that lead to unintended outcomes. Sex education efforts, particularly abstinence programs, have been ineffective at preventing hundreds of thousands of unintended pregnancies among teenagers each year, proving that some kind of change is necessary. According to a study by the University of Washington, "teenagers who received comprehensive sex education were 60 percent less likely to get pregnant than [those] who received abstinence-only education."[91] States with the highest teen pregnancy rates are the ones that teach abstinence-only education. When these teenagers discover they are pregnant, they face additional controversy over the decisions they make about what to do next.

CHAPTER 5

Important Decisions for Pregnant Teens

Pregnancy is always big news. Whether a woman is happy, uncertain, or unhappy about becoming pregnant is generally dependent on a number of factors, one of which is whether she was actively trying to become pregnant. Other factors may include her age, whether she is currently single or in a relationship, whether she is physically ready to have a child, and whether she can emotionally and financially care for a child. More than 75 percent of teen pregnancies are unplanned, so it is generally scary and overwhelming for a teen to discover that she is going to have a baby. Suddenly, this teen is faced with a number of complicated issues, such as how to tell the father of the child, whether to tell her parents, and what to do about the child. These are heavy topics for anyone to consider, and they are especially difficult for teenagers because of the negative stereotype that is associated with teen pregnancy in America. Typically, the young woman receives more scorn than the father of the child because of double standards in American society. Women are often looked down on for having sex, while men are congratulated. The mother is most often the one who is shamed for having sex and "getting herself pregnant;" she may be told that she should have made the decision not to have sex, while little mention may be made of the father and his role in the pregnancy. Men are more often criticized if they abandon the woman they had sex with and fail to support her and the child.

There are several choices that young women can make when they find out they are pregnant. They can choose to end the pregnancy by having an abortion or carry the pregnancy to term and give birth. If they give birth, they can choose whether to

Pregnant teens can choose to have an abortion, place their child for adoption, or keep and raise their child. There are many factors involved in this decision.

place the child for adoption or raise the baby, either on their own or with the father. All these choices have pros and cons, and the decision-making process is emotional and difficult. The physical, emotional, and financial consequences often feel harsher to teens because of the stigma associated with being a teen mom. Pressures from the media, friends, family, and the community all exert their influence, but ultimately, it is the young teen's choice. Approximately 15 percent of teen pregnancies end in miscarriage, but the other 85 percent of these girls will need to make one of the biggest decisions of their lives.

Abortion: A Hotly Debated Topic

Abortion is a medical method by which a woman can end her pregnancy. It has become one of the most controversial topics in the United States today. Various abortion options are available, which are all opposed by members of the pro-life movement. Before the 10th week of pregnancy, a woman can take medication that brings about a miscarriage. Abortion also can be performed by a surgical procedure that removes the embryo (what a developing baby is called in the first eight weeks of pregnancy) or the fetus (a developing baby nine or more weeks into pregnancy), along with the lining of the uterus. Surgical abortions are generally performed during the first 12 weeks of a pregnancy. Most abortions are considered outpatient procedures, which means that the patient does not need to be admitted to a hospital, but can have the procedure in a doctor's office or clinic and go home the same day. Medically, an abortion is a fairly straightforward process. Although there is a small risk that a woman who has an abortion will have trouble getting pregnant again later in life or will have trouble carrying a later pregnancy for the full term, abortions are generally considered to have few, if any, long-term physical consequences. Compared with being pregnant for a full nine months and the physical toll that pregnancy and childbirth can take on a teen's body, abortion is sometimes even considered a preferable option for some pregnant teens, at least in terms of physical health. According to specialists Barbara M. Newman and Philip R. Newman, "Legal abortion, especially before 12 weeks, [is] over 10 times safer physically than carrying a pregnancy to term." They added that legal abortion is "one of the safest surgical procedures in the United States."[92]

For many teenagers, abortion is an attractive choice for coping with an unplanned pregnancy because it also lessens or even eliminates the social stigma that a teen may feel or experience as a result of being pregnant. Many teens who discover they are pregnant feel embarrassed or ashamed and may wish to hide the pregnancy from their family, friends, or peers to the extent that they may want to drop out of school, run away from home, or make other choices that could have long-term negative effects on their lives. For some pregnant teens, abortion is a way to avoid the social stigma, and they may feel it is the best option available for them to complete their education and meet life goals. Tulalah, a woman who chose to have an

SINGLE MOMS STEP UP

"I don't ever see [my son's] father. He's only a year older than I am and he wasn't ready to be a father ... It was really hard for me to deal with having a baby without his support ... but the responsibility is all my own. I'm the mother; I have to care for my child."
—Renee, teenage mother

Quoted in Margi Trapani, *Listen Up! Teenage Mothers Speak Out.* New York, NY: Rosen, 2001, pp. 27-28.

abortion as a college freshman, wrote "I was just about to turn 19 and I was pregnant ... I knew that I could not have the child. Not because I didn't want children, but I was not ready to take the responsibility for another life when I couldn't really provide for myself."[93]

Abortions are generally safe when done by a doctor, but like any medical procedure, they can have negative side effects. The process can be painful, causing severe cramping and heavy bleeding from the woman's uterus. Complications, although rare, include infection, damage to the reproductive organs, and blood clots. Abortions are much more dangerous if, in an effort to hide the pregnancy and abortion from everyone, a teenager tries to induce an abortion by herself through methods such as taking dangerous substances to terminate her pregnancy.

There are many obstacles to abortion for women of all ages but particularly for teens. Because teenagers younger than 18 are still minors, in 38 states they are unable to have an abortion without their parents' knowledge or consent, making abortion a difficult option for a teen who does not want her parents to know she is pregnant. In those states, however, a judge or doctor can excuse the teen from having to get her parents' permission.

Another obstacle is the cost. Some states ban insurance coverage for abortions, but even in places where it is covered, teens who do not want their parents to know about their abortion may choose to pay out of pocket to avoid the insurance company sending their parents a bill. Abortions can cost anywhere from $300 to $1,200, so many teens cannot afford one. Additionally, even when the parents are supportive and agree to help their daughter pay through insurance, some insurance companies will refuse to participate.

Abortion is also sometimes viewed poorly by society. A woman who has an abortion may receive harsh treatment from other people if they know about the procedure because many Americans believe abortion is murder. Although the 1973 *Roe v. Wade* ruling by the U.S. Supreme Court legalized abortion and gave all women in the United States the right to end an unwanted pregnancy, the decision has been attacked ever since by people who oppose abortion. "Usually a Supreme Court decision marks the end of a long legal struggle," psychologist Simone Payment wrote. "In the case of *Roe v. Wade*, another fight was about to begin … Antiabortion groups quickly began organizing an attempt to overturn the Court's ruling."[94] Legal and social battles over *Roe v. Wade* have continued in the United States for decades. Because it is such an emotionally charged issue, women who choose abortion, even though they do so legally, may face a negative reaction from other people.

Due to the fact that the federal government declared abortion legal, states cannot ban it. However, state governments that oppose abortion get around this by making it extremely difficult for a woman to get the procedure. Some states require a woman to get counseling before she can have her abortion, and the woman may be given false information, including that abortions can cause breast cancer. Others require a waiting period in hopes that a woman will change her mind or not be able to get back to the clinic for her second appointment. In states such as Texas, laws for abortion clinics have been made so strict that many have to close, which means a woman may have to travel for hours to get to one. Teens who do not have access to a car or other transportation may not be able to get an abortion simply because they cannot get to a place that performs them.

In a society where the subject of abortion faces so much intense and fierce debate, teenagers who opt to have an abortion and are struggling emotionally with their decision may not feel they can talk about it openly before or after the fact. Girls who are pressured into having an abortion they did not want, have a history of depression even before getting pregnant, or believe they are doing something wrong by getting an abortion may experience guilt, shame, or depression afterward.

People who support a woman's right to get an abortion are called pro-choice. They believe women have the right to decide what happens to their bodies.

Many people claim that all women experience these negative emotions after an abortion, but according to the Guttmacher Institute in 2006, "it is fair to say that neither the weight of the scientific evidence to date nor the observable reality of 33 years of legal abortion in the United States [supports] the idea that having an abortion is any more dangerous to a woman's long-term mental health than delivering and parenting a child that she did not intend to have or placing a baby for adoption."[95]

An abortion is perhaps the most controversial of all the options a teenager has for dealing with an unplanned pregnancy, and many pregnant teenagers do not feel that abortion is right for them or that it is an accessible or practical choice. For these young women, continuing with a pregnancy and giving birth is the only other option. Their choices then come down to whether they will keep the baby or place him or her for adoption after the birth.

Adoption: A Tough Choice

Teens who learn they are pregnant tend to feel fear and uncertainty about the future. Few teens actively try to become pregnant; most regard pregnancy as an accident or even a mistake. However, approximately 59 percent of all pregnant teenagers do not have a miscarriage and do not opt for abortion, according to the Guttmacher Institute. The Guttmacher Institute also reported that in 2011, there were 13.5 abortions for every 1,000 women aged 15 to 19. This is the lowest rate observed since abortion was legalized in 1973, and it is 69 percent lower than the peak rate of 44.0 in 1988. Despite the fact that the pregnancy may have been unexpected or even unwanted, many teens choose to remain pregnant and ultimately give birth. These expectant mothers often face difficult decisions about what to do during pregnancy and after the baby arrives. Most pregnant teenagers realize that delaying or quitting school will make life harder later on, yet continuing to go to class can be challenging for a pregnant teenager who is still in high school. The physical changes her body undergoes during pregnancy may make her too tired to study, for example, and the changes to her appearance eventually become noticeable to other people, which can make her feel self-conscious or expose her to stares, gossip, and ridicule. She may even feel pressured by peers or adults to drop out of school during her pregnancy.

Facing the challenges of life as a teenage parent—a life in which many freedoms vanish and responsibilities increase dramatically—some pregnant teenagers decide that placing the baby for adoption after it is born is the best choice, both for them and their baby. Most who make this decision cite two reasons: They realize that raising a child will make it difficult to achieve their own goals and hopes for the future, and they also realize that as a teenager, with or without the help of the baby's father, they can provide fewer advantages for the child than adoptive parents who are older and whose lives are more stable. Susan, a teenage mother who made the choice to let someone adopt her baby, said "At age sixteen, the last thing on my mind was becoming pregnant and facing decisions like adoption … I knew right away that it would not have been possible for me to provide the home that a child deserves. And I was not willing to make it my parents' responsibility."[96]

Adoption is widely considered a good option for pregnant teenagers, especially those who know they cannot or do not want to raise a child but who do not want to have an abortion. Expectant teenage parents who decide on adoption often say they have made a choice to put their baby's needs ahead of their own. Others are motivated both by their baby's needs and an evaluation of their own limitations and of how life would be if they kept and raised a baby. Shana, a teenage mother who placed her baby for adoption, said, "I wasn't interested in spending my life on welfare (or raising my baby that way) … I felt my child deserved more than spending his or her life in daycare, while I worked full-time (or more) to make ends meet." For teenage parents such as Shana, adoption is a positive solution to a difficult situation. As Shana explained, "The entire decision has brought me much joy and peace."[97]

On the other hand, adoption is not without its downside. Unlike pregnant teenagers who opt for abortion, a pregnant teen who plans to place her baby for adoption still faces the possible physical challenges of pregnancy to which teenagers are more susceptible. Placing a child for adoption may also have negative emotional effects on the teenage parents. Many teenage parents say the decision to place their baby for adoption is a difficult decision, even if they believe they are doing the best thing for themselves and for their child. Katharine, a 16-year-old who placed her baby for adoption, said, "The father and I knew we couldn't give our wonderful baby everything she needed or wanted … It was the hardest thing we've ever done. Probably the hardest thing we'll ever do."[98] Some teenage parents who

Same-sex couples sometimes choose to adopt children, and they can provide a stable adoptive family for a baby born to teenagers.

A Not-So-Realistic Happy Ending

The movie *Juno*, released in 2007, told the story of a fictional 16-year-old who got pregnant and placed her baby for adoption. The film was advertised as a romantic comedy and had a happy ending. It was nominated for four Oscars, but it was also widely criticized for giving an unrealistic picture of the consequences of teen pregnancy because Juno's baby was adopted, and the teen moved on with life as if little had changed. In reality, though, only 2 percent of women actually place their babies for adoption. The movie also was criticized because Juno came from a supportive family, when a majority of pregnant teenagers statistically have underprivileged lifestyles and do not feel supported emotionally or financially at home. However, others felt that this was not a problem because some pregnant teens do have parents who support them through their pregnancy, so it was not necessarily a false portrayal. *Juno* was accused of romanticizing teen pregnancy and showing it as quirky and not very serious. The movie's screenwriter, Diablo Cody, said she was not trying to write a movie about teen pregnancy, but rather one about relationships. The movie was not necessarily meant to be factual or realistic, nor was it intended to teach a teen audience right from wrong. Nevertheless, the controversy surrounding *Juno* reflected the varied opinions about pregnant teens and how the media depicts them.

The 2007 move Juno *sparked much controversy about teenage mothers and adoption.*

have placed a child for adoption even say they have lived with regret over that decision. They are more likely to feel this way if they are pressured into giving up a child they want to keep. Laurie Frisch, a woman who, as a teenager, placed her daughter for adoption, said, "I did not do the 'loving thing' as much as I did the 'uninformed thing' ... I was led to believe that giving away a child would be more like giving away a puppy than actually losing your closest family member ... I was told I would 'get over it.'... I never will."[99]

Although adoption is often considered a good choice both for a teenage mother and her child, it is the least common choice pregnant teens make when deciding what to do about their pregnancy. In fact, only about 2 percent of teenage mothers choose to place their child for adoption. Lois gave birth to a daughter at age 15 and chose to be a single teenage mom. She raised her child to be a happy, healthy, college-bound young woman—a success story that shows that teenagers can make good parents. She said, "I sometimes wonder how [my daughter] would've turned out had she become another woman's child at one day of age ... I honestly don't know if I would've survived without [her] in my life all these years."[100] It is a sentiment that most pregnant teenagers seem to share because very few make the choice to part with their child. The majority of teens who become pregnant in the United States give birth to and raise their babies.

Kids Raising Kids

Becoming a parent can be an exciting and positive event, no matter what age the parents are. Some studies have shown that approximately 20 percent of all teen pregnancies occur among young women who claim to want a child and who either intend to become pregnant or have said they would not be upset to learn they were pregnant. Some of these young women are in love with the father of their child; others simply want a baby. Even among the teen pregnancies that are not intentional, the mother often chooses to keep her child. A 21-year-old identified only as K. told *TIME*, "It's hard for me to get a job, so now I'm being supported by my mother. Don't get me wrong, children are the greatest gift you can ever have, but in all honesty it's

Despite the hardships, many teen mothers provide good lives for their children.

pretty hard as a teenage mother. If I had a chance to wait 'til I was stable, I would take it."[101]

Having a child is always a life-changing event and can be a considerable challenge for any parent, both financially and emotionally. For teenagers, the difficulties and stresses of parenthood are often made worse by their age. Depending on how old the mother and father are when the baby arrives, they may still be legal minors, which makes it difficult to find a place to live because they may not yet be legally able to rent. Some teenage parents are not even old enough to drive, or they may not be

Teen Dads

Although it is common for the fathers to be several years older than the teenage mothers, many dads are still teenagers themselves. Society sometimes stereotypes teenage fathers as reckless, promiscuous, and unwilling to take responsibility for supporting their children. Teenage mothers are often portrayed as being left behind to raise a child while teenage fathers go on with life as usual. However, research on teen dads has shown that these stereotypes are rarely true. A nationwide study in 2005 by New York City's Bank Street College of Education found that 75 percent of teenage fathers contributed financially to raising their child, and more than 80 percent saw their child almost every day. Although the rate of teen fatherhood "declined 54% between 1991 and 2014, from 25 to 11 per 1,000 males aged 15–19,"[1] teen fathers still drop out of school in order to work full time to help with child expenses. Because education is so important to getting a good job that can support a family, providing teenage fathers with assistance and opportunities for staying in school could be one way to lessen the financial burden of parenthood for teenage mothers and fathers alike.

Many teen dads step up to help raise their children.

1. "American Teens' Sexual and Reproductive Health," Guttmacher Institute, September 2016. www.guttmacher.org/fact-sheet/american-teens-sexual-and-reproductive-health#21.

A VICIOUS CYCLE

"My father was a parent when he was a
teenager. My mother and grandmother were.
It didn't stop with me or with my brothers. I
know it will stop with my son."
—Terry, teenage father

Quoted in Richard Stengel, "Teenage Fathers: The Missing-Father Myth," *TIME*, June 21, 2005.
www.time.com/time/magazine/article/0,9171,1074862-2,00.html#xzz11QlxxTWD.

able to afford a car, gas, vehicle maintenance, car insurance, and other expenses related to driving. Without transportation, they may not be able to get to and from day care and work or school, which makes it difficult or impossible to keep a job or complete a high school education. Many teenage parents depend on support from family members to make ends meet, to have a place to live, and to continue to pursue goals such as education. This often means that the new baby's other relatives, such as grandparents, aunts, and uncles, take on at least some of the financial and time burdens of raising the baby. Although some teenage mothers do marry or live with the father of their child, many are single and often lack financial contributions from the father, who may claim he is not the one responsible for the child or who may not make enough money to help much with the costs of raising the child.

As desperate as the financial situation may be for many teenage parents and especially single teenage mothers, there are resources to help. Young mothers can apply for and receive government assistance. There are also increasing resources for teenage mothers in many communities. Community health services often help provide basic but essential medical care for the child, such as vaccines and checkups, generally at a lower cost than private doctors. Child care is also provided in some public high schools to give young mothers the opportunity to obtain a high school diploma that will help them get a better job. These resources, however, are opposed by many Americans

Being a teenage parent is challenging, but it does not change the love a mother can feel for her child.

who believe that public services should not be available to teenage parents at taxpayers' cost and may even think teenage mothers are using such resources to avoid adult responsibility. However, the Affordable Care Act (ACA) legislation is changing the way that health care is handled in the United States. Health insurance coverage and the ability to pay for services affects teens' access to reproductive health care. Prior to many of the ACA insurance coverage benefits taking effect, approximately 27.2 percent of young adults 19 to 25 years old were uninsured,

Avoiding Homelessness

Teenage girls living in poverty are the most likely of all teenagers to become pregnant, and pregnancy adds economic hardship to their lives, especially if they find themselves homeless. This is the case for many teens, such as those in foster homes (many of which will not house pregnant teens), those whose family has kicked them out because of the pregnancy, or those who were already homeless when they became pregnant. Group homes for pregnant teenagers and new teen mothers are a source of help. These government-funded facilities exist around the country and are safe places where teenagers can go to live during and after pregnancy. In return for shelter and food, teens who live in such homes are expected to make progress toward independence through work, school, classes on parenting and life skills, and household chores, such as cleaning, cooking, and grocery shopping. These group homes often have strict rules, including curfews, early morning wake-up calls, and restrictions on visitors. Living there may not always be easy, but admission is competitive nonetheless because the homes give teens who are pregnant or are already mothers a temporary place to live and an opportunity to prepare for independent life.

and 15 percent were covered by Medicaid—government-sponsored health insurance for low-income citizens—in 2012. About 6 out of 10 young adults (61 percent) lived in a low-income household (below 200 percent of the federal poverty level). After the initial insurance enrollment period in 2014, the uninsured rate among young adults ages 18 to 25 has declined to 18.7 percent. Access to health care for teens has helped provide better care for them and their babies.

Welfare is still an option for young mothers who are struggling financially. However, resources such as welfare are not without drawbacks for teenage parents. If a young mother receives welfare benefits, they often come at their own cost to her. She is required to put her baby in a child care situation and work to supplement the welfare income as much as she can. Some young women also feel like it is a bad thing to rely on welfare. Not all young parents are able to pursue educational goals to try to secure a better future for themselves and their children. For many, pregnancy and parenthood at a young age do lead to a life of poverty and contribute to what has been identified as a poverty cycle: Girls who were born to teenage mothers are more likely to become mothers as teenagers themselves, and children born into poverty are more likely to remain in poverty once they are adults.

The Discussion Continues

Despite the recent decline in the teen pregnancy rate, the issue of young people having children before they can support them will continue to be a topic of debate in the United States. There are many aspects to consider, including the discussion of teen pregnancy being a public health or social issue, teenage promiscuity, the portrayal of sex in the media, and the degree to which sex education should be taught in public schools. However, perhaps the most important issues of this debate to consider are the life of the teen mother and her child and how to ensure that we as a society are properly caring for both. Helping teenagers make appropriate and responsible choices about their lives may be the best and most important way to continue to decrease the teen pregnancy rate. Lowering the number of teenagers getting pregnant will help society in many ways, and it will also help improve the lives of many young girls and children.

Introduction: A Social Problem on the Decline

1. "Teenage Pregnancy and Birth Rates—United States, 1990," Centers for Disease Control and Prevention, October 1, 1993. www.cdc.gov/mmwr/preview/mmwrhtml/00021930.htm.

Chapter 1: What Causes Teen Pregnancy?

2. "Trends in High School Dropout and Completion Rates in the United States," National Center for Education Statistics, 2011. nces.ed.gov/pubs2012/2012006.pdf.

3. Billy Hallowell, "What Americans Really Believe About the State of Morality in the U.S," The Blaze, June 4, 2015. www.theblaze. com/stories/2015/06/04/is-america-in-a-moral-decline-liber-als-and-conservatives-reveal-their-views-on-the-state-of-the-nations-ethics/.

4. Kerby Anderson, "The Teen Sexual Revolution," Leadership U, 2003. www.leaderU.com/orgs/probe/docs/sexrevol.html.

5. Quoted in Good Morning America, "Teens Speak Out on Palin's Pregnancy: GMA Hosts a Roundtable to Get Teens' Thoughts on Sex, Pregnancy," September 4, 2008. abcnews.go.com/GMA/story?id=5725586&page=1.

6. Quoted in Good Morning America, "Teens Speak Out on Palin's Pregnancy."

7. Saul D. Hoffman and Rebecca A. Maynard, eds., Kids Having Kids: Economic Costs and Social Consequences of Teen Pregnancy, 2nd ed. Washington, DC: Urban Institute, 2008, p. 4.

8. "Pregnancy and Childbearing Among U.S. Teens," Planned Parenthood Federation of America, 2014. www.planned parenthood.org/files/2013/9611/7570/Pregnancy_And_Childbearing_Among_US_Teens.pdf.

9. Quoted in Tara Parker-Pope, "The Myth of Rampant Teenage Promiscuity," *New York Times*, January 26, 2009, p. D6.

10. Guttmacher Institute, *Can More Progress Be Made? Teenage Sexual and Reproductive Behaviors in Developed Countries*. Washington, DC: Guttmacher Institute, 2001, p. 6. www.guttmacher.org/pubs/eurosynth_rpt.pdf.

11. Quoted in Rob Stein, "Rise in Teenage Pregnancy Rate Spurs New Debate on Arresting It," *Washington Post*, January 26, 2010. www.washingtonpost.com/wp-dyn/content/article/2010/01/25/AR2010012503957.html.

12. Daniel Hart and Gustavo Carlo, "Moral Development in Adolescence," *Journal of Research on Adolescence*, vol. 15, no. 3, 2005, p. 224.

13. Andrew L. Cherry, Mary E. Dillon, and Douglas Rugh, eds., *Teenage Pregnancy: A Global View*. Westport, CT: Greenwood, 2001, pp. xii, xiv.

14. Guttmacher Institute, *Can More Progress Be Made?*, p. 69.

15. Frederica Mathewes-Green, "Let's Have More Teen Pregnancy," *National Review*, September 20, 2002. www.frederica.com/writings/lets-have-more-teen-pregnancy.html.

16. Cherry, Dillon, and Rugh, eds., *Teenage Pregnancy*, p. xv.

17. Guttmacher Institute, *Can More Progress Be Made?*, p. 4.

18. Marty Klein, *America's War on Sex: The Attack on Law, Lust, and Liberty*. Westport, CT: Praeger, 2006, p. 24.

19. Quoted in Sabrina Weill, *The Real Truth About Teens & Sex*. New York, NY: Penguin, 2005, p. 104.

20. Guttmacher Institute, *Can More Progress Be Made?*, p. 2.

21. G. Martinez, C. E. Copen, and J. C. Abma, "Teenagers in the United States: Sexual Activity, Contraceptive Use, and Childbearing, 2006-2010 National Survey of Family Growth," *Vital and Health Statistics*, 2011, series 23, no. 31, p. 27.

22. Nancy Gibbs, "Why Have Abortion Rates Fallen?" *TIME*, January 12, 2008. www.time.com/time/nation/article/0,8599,1705604,00.html.

23. Quoted in Gibbs, "Why Have Abortion Rates Fallen?"

24. Diane J. MacUnovich, "Baby Boomers," *Encyclopedia of Aging*, 2002. www.encyclopedia.com/doc/1G2-3402200042.html.

25. Mathewes-Green, "Let's Have More Teen Pregnancy."

26. Family Connection of St. Joseph County, "Teenage Pregnancy," 1996. community.michiana.org/famconn/teenpreg.html.

27. Klein, *America's War on Sex*, p. 6.

Chapter 2: The Far-Reaching Effects of Teen Pregnancy

28. Quoted in Lawrence S. Neinstein, ed., *Adolescent Health Care: A Practical Guide*, 5th ed. Philadelphia, PA: Lippincott, Williams & Wilkins, 2008, p. 574.

29. Nancy T. Hatfield, *Broadribb's Introductory Pediatric Nursing*, 7th ed. Philadelphia, PA: Lippincott, Williams & Wilkins, 2007, p. 618.

30. Stacy C. Hodgkinson et al., "Depressive Symptoms and Birth Outcomes Among Pregnant Teenagers," *Journal of Pediatric and Adolescent Gynecology*, vol. 23, no. 1, February 2010, pp. 16–22. doi.org/10.1016/j.jpag.2009.04.006.

31. Jonathan D. Klein, "Adolescent Pregnancy: Current Trends and Issues," *Pediatrics*, vol. 116, no. 1, 2005, p. 285.

32. Steven Maddocks, *United Nations Children's Fund Worldwatch Series*. Chicago, IL: Raintree, 2004, p. 20.

33. Barbara Luke, *Every Pregnant Woman's Guide to Preventing Premature Birth*. Lincoln, NE: Authors Choice, 2002, pp. 4–5.

34. Jeffrey Roth et al., "The Risk of Teen Mothers Having Low Birth Weight Babies: Implications of Recent Medical Research for School Health Personnel," *Journal of School Health*, vol. 68, no. 7, 1998, pp. 272, 274.

35. "Teen Pregnancy," Child Trends, April 2016. www.childtrends.org/?indicators=teen-pregnancy.

36. Nweze Eunice Nnakwe, *Community Nutrition: Planning Health Promotion and Disease Prevention*. Sudbury, MA: Jones and Bartlett, 2009, p. 154.

37. Kathleen Sylvester, *Teenage Pregnancy: A Preventable Calamity*. Washington, DC: Progressive Policy Institute, 1994, pp. 1–2.

38. National Campaign to Prevent Teen and Unplanned Pregnancy, "Why It Matters: The Costs of Teen Childbearing." www.thenationalcampaign.org/why-it-matters/pdf/costs.pdf.

39. Debbie A. Lawlor and Mary Shaw, "What a Difference a Year Makes? Too Little Too Late," *International Journal of Epidemiology*, vol. 31, 2002, p. 558.

40. Lisa Arai, *Teenage Pregnancy: The Making and Unmaking of a Problem*. Bristol, UK: Policy, 2009, p. 9.

41. Lawlor and Shaw, "What a Difference a Year Makes?" p. 558.

Chapter 3: Teen Pregnancy and Society

42. Arai, *Teenage Pregnancy*, p. 49.

43. Alan Cribb and Peter Duncan, *Health Promotion and Professional Ethics*. Oxford, UK: Blackwell, 2002, p. 67.

44. Arai, *Teenage Pregnancy*, p. 39.

45. Arai, *Teenage Pregnancy*, pp. 39–40.

46. Sharon Lynn Nichols and Thomas L. Good, *America's Teenagers—Myths and Realities: Media Images, Schooling, and the Social Costs of Careless Indifference*. Mahwah, NJ: Lawrence Erlbaum, 2004, p. 92.

47. Nichols and Good, *America's Teenagers*, p. 96.

48. Nichols and Good, *America's Teenagers*, p. 96.

49. Nichols and Good, *America's Teenagers*, p. 84.

50. Rebecca L. Collins et al., "Watching Sex on Television Predicts Adolescent Initiation of Sexual Behavior," *Pediatrics*, vol. 114, 2004, p. e281. pediatrics.aappublications.org/cgi/reprint/114/3/e280.

51. Nichols and Good, *America's Teenagers*, p. 92.

52. Quoted in Allan M. Brandt and Paul Rozin, eds., *Morality and Health*. London, UK: Routledge, 1997, p. 252.

53. Genevieve Martinez-Garcia et al., "Do Latino Youth Really Want to Get Pregnant?" Healthy Teen Network, 2014. www.healthyteennetwork.org/under-the-currents/do-latino-youth-really-want-get-pregnant.

54. Teresa Wiltz, "Racial and Ethnic Disparities Persist in Teen Pregnancy Rates," The Pew Charitable Trusts, March 3, 2015. www.pewtrusts.org/en/research-and-analysis/blogs/stateline/2015/3/03/racial-and-ethnic-disparities-persist-in-teen-pregnancy-rates.

55. Quoted in Lauren Wicks, "Breaking Down the Statistics: Teen Pregnancy Especially Prevalent Among African-Americans," *Suffolk News-Herald*, September 2, 2009. www.suffolknewsherald.com/news/2009/sep/02/breaking-down-statistics/.

56. Steven Emery-Wright, *Understanding Teenage Sexuality: A Foundation for Christian Relationships*. Singapore: Genesis, 2009, pp. 102–103.

57. Mark D. Regnerus, *Forbidden Fruit: Sex and Religion in the Lives of American Teenagers*. New York, NY: Oxford University Press, 2007, p. 184.

58. Marlena Studer and Arland Thornton, "Adolescent Religiosity and Contraceptive Usage," *Journal of Marriage and the Family*, vol. 49, no. 1, February 1987, p. 117-128.

59. Barbara Miller, *Teen Pregnancy and Poverty: The Economic Realities*. New York, NY: Rosen, 1997, p. 31.

60. Cherry, Dillon, and Rugh, eds., *Teenage Pregnancy*, p. xii.

61. Quoted in Sana Loue and Beth E. Quill, eds., *Handbook of Rural Health*. New York, NY: Kluwer Academic/Plenum, 2001, p. 41.

62. Frank D. Cox, *Human Intimacy: Marriage, the Family, and Its Meaning*, 10th ed. Belmont, CA: Wadsworth, 2009, p. 258.

63. Anne L. Dean, *Teenage Pregnancy: The Interaction of Psyche and Culture*. Hillsdale, NJ: Analytic, 1997, p. xiii.

64. Cribb and Duncan, *Health Promotion and Professional Ethics*, p. 72.

Chapter 4: Decreasing the Teen Pregnancy Rate

65. Charles Zastrow and Karen K. Kirst-Ashman, *Understanding Human Behavior and the Social Environment*, 8th ed. Belmont, CA: Brooks/Cole, 2010, p. 267.

66. Quoted in Sarah Kershaw, "Now, the Bad News on Teenage Marriage," *New York Times*, September 4, 2008, p. G1.

67. Quoted in Kershaw, "Now, the Bad News on Teenage Marriage," p. G1.

68. Maggie Gallagher, *The Age of Unwed Mothers: Is Teen Pregnancy the Problem?: A Report to the Nation*. New York, NY: Institute for American Values, 1999, p. 3.

69. U.S. Department of Health and Human Services, *Healthy People 2010*, 2nd ed., vol. 1. Washington, DC: U.S. Government Printing Office, 2000, section 9, p. 5.

70. Lynne Collenback, "Why I Choose Abstinence," *San Angelo Abstinence Examiner*, June 4, 2010. www.examiner.com/x-52012-San-Angelo-Abstinence-Examiner~y2010m6d4-Why-I-Choose-Abstinence.

71. Quoted in Choosing the Best Publishing, "New Figures Show Abstinence Emphasis Working," press release, April 10, 2001. www.choosingthebest.org/press_room/press_ release_1.htm.

72. Quoted in Choosing the Best Publishing, "New Figures Show Abstinence Emphasis Working."

73. Klein, *America's War on Sex*, pp. 21–22.

74. Rachel Sanoff, "7 Problems With the State of Sex Ed in America Today, and How We Can Make It Better," *Bustle*, August 27, 2015. www.bustle.com/articles/104233-7-problems-with-the-state-of-sex-ed-in-america-today-and-how-we-can-make.

75. Margaret O. Hyde and Elizabeth H. Forsyth, *Safe Sex 101: An Overview for Teens*. Minneapolis, MN: Twenty-First Century, 2006, pp. 63–64.

76. John Santelli et al., "Abstinence and Abstinence-Only Education: A Review of U.S. Policies and Programs," *Journal of Adolescent Health*, vol. 38, 2006, p. 79.

77. Quoted in Sabrina Weill, *The Real Truth About Teens & Sex: From Hooking Up to Friends with Benefits—What Teens Are Thinking, Doing, and Talking About and How to Help Them Make Smart Choices*. New York, NY: Penguin, 2005, p. 21.

78. Kaiser Family Foundation, *National Survey of Adolescents and Young Adults: Sexual Health Knowledge, Attitudes, and Experiences*. Menlo Park, CA: Kaiser Family Foundation, 2003, p. 2. kaiserfamilyfoundation.files.wordpress.com/2013/01/national-

survey-of-adolescents-and-young-adults.pdf.

79. Emma Elliott, *What Your Teacher Didn't Tell You About Abstinence*. Washington, DC: Concerned Women for America, 2005. concernedwomen.org/wp-content/uploads/2013/11/cwa_abstinence_brochure.pdf.

80. Keri J. Dodd, "School Condom Availability," Advocates for Youth, February 1998. www.advocatesforyouth.org/publications/449-school-condom-availability.

81. American College of Pediatricians, "Abstinence Education." www.acpeds.org/the-college-speaks/position-statements/sexuality-issues/abstinence-education.

82. Amy Gutmann, *Democratic Education*. Princeton, NJ: Princeton University Press, 1987, p. 111.

83. Clint Bruess and Jerrold Greenberg, *Sexuality Education: Theory and Practice*, 5th ed. Sudbury, MA: Jones and Bartlett, 2009, p. 31.

84. Bruess and Greenberg, *Sexuality Education*, p. 32.

85. Lisa H. Warren, "Understanding the Conservative Positions on Sex Education," Helium. www.helium.com/items/721779-understanding-the-conservative-positions-on-sex-education.

86. Quoted in Sanoff, "7 Problems With the State of Sex Ed."

87. Gutmann, *Democratic Education*, p. 110.

88. Quoted in "One Teen's Opinion: Why Sex Education Is Important," Family Education. life.familyeducation.com/sex/teen/36177.html.

89. Quoted in Sylvia Magora, "Young Activists Passionate About Pregnancy Prevention," MTV News, *Sex Etc.*, May 5, 2005. www.mtv.com/onair/ffyr/protect/sexetc_may_05.jhtml.

90. Courtney E. Martin, "Willful Ignorance," *The American Prospect*, January 17, 2007. prospect.org/article/willful-ignorance-0.

91. Matt Essert, "The States With the Highest Teenage Birth Rates Have One Thing in Common," Mic, September 15, 2014. mic.com/articles/98886/the-states-with-the-highest-teenage-birth-rates-have-one-thing-in-common#.HnpB30T59.

Chapter 5: Important Decisions for Pregnant Teens

92. Barbara M. Newman and Philip R. Newman, *Development Through Life: A Psychosocial Approach*, 10th ed. Belmont, CA: Wadsworth Cengage Learning, 2009, p. 125.

93. Quoted in Feminist Women's Health Center, "Tulalah's Story," February 2, 1999. www.fwhc.org/stories/tulalah.htm.

94. Simone Payment, *Supreme Court Cases Through Primary Sources: Roe v. Wade, the Right to Choose*. New York, NY: Rosen, 2004, pp. 47–48.

95. Susan A. Cohen, "Abortion and Mental Health: Myths and Realities," Guttmacher Institute, August 1, 2006. www.guttmacher.org/about/gpr/2006/08/abortion-and-mental-health-myths-and-realities.

96. Quoted in Independent Adoption Center, "Susan's Story: I've Been Given a Chance to Pursue My Goals." www.adoptionhelp.org/birthmother/stories/susan.html.

97. Quoted in Independent Adoption Center, "Shana's Story: I Will Never Regret My Choice." www.adoptionhelp.org/birthmother/stories/shana.html.

98. Quoted in Independent Adoption Center, "Katharine's Story: I'm So Thankful for Open Adoption." www.adoptionhelp.org/birthmother/stories/katharine.html.

99. Laurie Frisch, "A Personal Adoption Story," *A Mother's Song: Taking the Crisis out of Pregnancy*, 2003. www.motherhelp.info/about_me.htm.

100. Quoted in *A Mother's Song: Taking the Crisis out of Pregnancy*, "Adoption or Teen Parenting?" www.motherhelp.info/adoption_letter.htm.

101. Belinda Luscombe, "Teens Answer: Why I Had a Baby," *TIME*, February 3, 2011. healthland.time.com/2011/02/03/teens-answer-why-i-had-a-baby/.

Chapter 1: What Causes Teen Pregnancy?

1. What do you think are the main causes of teen pregnancy in the United States?

2. Do you see the effects of teen pregnancy at your school or in your community? If so, what are some of the things you notice?

3. What, in your opinion, is the most likely reason why teen pregnancy rates are higher in the United States than in other developed countries?

Chapter 2: The Far-Reaching Effects of Teen Pregnancy

1. Do you think teen pregnancy is a public health problem? How would you support your answer?

2. Do you feel the U.S. government should be required to provide aid to pregnant teens and their children? Why or why not?

3. Why do you think the health risks of pregnant teenagers are frequently cited by the media when health risks of pregnancy among women older than age 40 are not?

Chapter 3: Teen Pregnancy and Society

1. Teen pregnancy rates are higher among Latinas, African Americans, and Native Americans than among whites. Why do you think this is the case? What might be done in the United States to deal with this difference?

2. Alan Cribb and Peter Duncan ask whether pregnancy

might be a positive choice—an expression of personal independence or a means of becoming fulfilled—for teenagers. What is your opinion?

3. Do you believe in abstaining from sex until marriage? Why or why not?

Chapter 4: Decreasing the Teen Pregnancy Rate

1. What are some advantages and disadvantages of abstinence-only, abstinence-plus, and comprehensive sex education programs? Which do you think is most successful at preventing teen pregnancy, and why?

2. What do you think teenagers need and want to learn in sex education programs?

3. Do you believe that sex education should be taught in schools, or is it the parents' responsibility to teach their children about sex?

Chapter 5: Important Decisions for Pregnant Teens

1. The author writes that a pregnant teenager faces three choices: abortion, adoption, or keeping and raising the baby. What are some pros and cons to each choice that may not have been discussed in the book?

2. The Supreme Court's decision in *Roe v. Wade* made abortion legal in the United States. What is your opinion about *Roe v. Wade*? How accessible do you think abortion should be to teens under age 18?

3. Do you believe teenagers are old enough to be parents? Why or why not?

ORGANIZATIONS TO CONTACT

Advocates for Youth
2000 M St. NW
Suite 750
Washington, DC 20036
Phone: (202) 419-3420
Website: www.advocatesforyouth.org
This organization provides information and resources for teenagers, parents, teachers, and youth advocates on sex education, teen pregnancy, abortion, and childbearing, all from a perspective of youths' rights.

American Congress of Obstetricians and Gynecologists
PO Box 70620
Washington, DC 20024
Phone: (800) 673-8444
Website: www.acog.org
The American Congress of Obstetricians and Gynecologists provides accurate information and the latest research about pregnancy and women's sexual health. The website has specific information and resources about teen pregnancy, informational booklets, and more.

American Pregnancy Association
1425 Greenway Dr.
Suite 440
Irving, TX 75038
Phone: (972) 550-0140
Toll-free: (800) 672-2296
Website: www.americanpregnancy.org
This organization offers access to pregnancy information and support, including a free, confidential hotline.

Guttmacher Institute

1301 Connecticut Ave. NW
Suite 700
Washington, DC 20036
Phone: (202) 296-4012
Toll-free: (877) 823-0262
Website: www.guttmacher.org
The aim of the Guttmacher Institute is to advance sexual and reproductive health worldwide through research and education. It is one of the U.S. government's leading providers of research and statistics on the nation's teen pregnancy trends.

Healthy Teen Network

1501 Saint Paul St.
Suite 124
Baltimore, MD 21202
Phone: (410) 685-0410
Website: www.healthyteennetwork.org
The Healthy Teen Network is a national organization focused on adolescent health and well-being with an emphasis on teen pregnancy prevention, pregnancy, and parenting.

Books

Englander, Anrenee. *Dear Diary, I'm Pregnant: Teenagers Talk About Pregnancy*. Rev. ed. Toronto, ON: Annick, 2010.
Ten teenagers relate stories of their experiences with pregnancy, giving a personal perspective of real young women faced with this complicated issue.

Haskins-Bookser, Laura. *Dreams to Reality: Help for Young Moms: Education, Career, and Life Choices*. Buena Park, CA: Morning Glory Press, 2006.
The author gives information about how young moms can continue their lives and achieve their dreams after having a child.

Lindsay, Jeanne Warren. *Teen Dads: Rights, Responsibilities & Joys*. Buena Park, CA: Morning Glory Press, 2008.
This book provides information, particularly for young men, on options surrounding teen pregnancy, family planning, and the experience of parenthood. It supplements the many books directed at teenage girls and their options for preventing or dealing with a pregnancy.

Rodriguez, Gaby. *The Pregnancy Project*. New York, NY: Simon and Schuster, 2012.
The author details her experience of faking a pregnancy to see how people would treat her differently when they thought she was going to be a teen mom.

Shantz-Hilkes, Chloe. *My Girlfriend's Pregnant!: A Teen's Guide to Becoming a Dad*. New York, NY: Annick Press, 2015.
Interviews with social workers, teen dads, and doctors give helpful information about what a teen can expect when he finds out his

girlfriend is pregnant. In addition to concrete solutions to a variety of challenges, this book discusses the many emotions an expectant teen dad may be feeling.

Websites

It's Your Sex Life

www.itsyoursexlife.com

Through a partnership between MTV and the Kaiser Family Foundation, this website offers up-to-date information about pregnancy prevention, resources for teens who are pregnant, a place to have a live chat with Planned Parenthood experts, and information about STDs.

Medline Plus

www.nlm.nih.gov/medlineplus/teenagepregnancy.html

In the "Teenage Pregnancy" section, Medline Plus, a service of the National Institutes of Health, offers accurate medical information about different aspects of teen pregnancy as well as links to helpful websites, journal articles, and more.

The National Campaign to Prevent Teen and
Unplanned Pregnancy

www.thenationalcampaign.org

Information about planning pregnancies—including data, consequences of teenage pregnancy, and public policy—is presented in an easy-to-read format on this website.

Planned Parenthood

www.plannedparenthood.org

In addition to helping people of all ages understand how to avoid an unwanted pregnancy and STDs, Planned Parenthood gives information about emotionally healthy relationships, health concerns for both men and women, and how gender identity influences people in their daily lives. Walk-in health clinics can be located by zip code on the site.

Scarleteen

www.scarleteen.com

For teens who feel that their sex education classes are not answering all their questions, Scarleteen has advice columns on topics such as birth control, sexual autonomy, creating a healthy relationship, issues that affect the LGBT community, and more. A live chat is available, and readers can submit their questions to the advice columnists.

Women's Health Channel

www.womenshealthchannel.com/teenpregnancy/index.shtml

In the section titled "Teen Pregnancy," this website discusses the health issues of pregnant teenagers, teen mothers, and their babies, along with information on birth control, teen pregnancy resources, and personal accounts from pregnant teens.

INDEX

PICTURE CREDITS

ABOUT THE AUTHOR

Emily Mahoney is the author of more than a dozen nonfiction books for young readers on various topics. She has a master's degree in literacy from the University at Buffalo and a bachelor's degree from Canisius College in adolescent education and English. She currently teaches reading to middle school students and loves watching her students learn how to become better readers and writers. She enjoys reading, pilates, yoga, and spending time with family and friends. She lives with her husband in Buffalo, New York, where she was born and raised.